Scandal of Grace

THE DANGER OF FOLLOWING JESUS

Nick Baines

SAINT ANDREW PRESS
Edinburgh

First published in 2004 as *Jesus and People Like Us* by
SAINT ANDREW PRESS
121 George Street
Edinburgh EH2 4YN

This edition published 2008

ISBN 978 0 7152 0866 3

British Library Cataloguing in Publication Data
A catalogue record for this book is available from the British Library

Typeset by Waverley Typesetters, Fakenham
Printed and bound by Bell & Bain Limited, Glasgow

CONTENTS

INTRODUCTION

'Journey' has possibly become an over-used metaphor in much recent Christian writing and preaching. However, it is still powerful because it is dynamic, not static. Also, as the Christian community reads and re-reads the Bible, God constantly appears as one who does not stand still. Furthermore, he seems constantly to be beckoning his people to move out and move on. He sometimes has to force their hand either by circumstance or by disappearing and absenting himself for a while.

This book is not an academic treatise on the nature of the cross and resurrection. Rather, it is born out of compulsive reading and hearing of the gospel narratives. I have lived with them, been shaped by them, been challenged by them and have tried to live them and teach them. They never turn dry, and they constantly surprise me by what they show of God, his Christ and his people. They concern people like me, and in their honesty and integrity I find space for my own fallibility and fecklessness. I also find I need no longer hide or pretend. For these narratives tell a story that is essentially liberating and deeply encouraging. Why? Because they give an insight into the nature and affections of a God who loves so deeply that he will risk everything for his world and his people.

This book is shaped simply to take us on a journey with the friends of Jesus as they go from a beach in Galilee to a gallows outside Jerusalem three years later. As we accompany them, we can listen in and reflect on some of what was happening. The temptation to apply every reflection to particular individuals or churches has to be resisted because that limits my expectation of the readers (that they will think for themselves and make their own connections) and fixes my own thinking in too particular a way. It is enough for my reflections to suggest how current controversies and questions might be seen in the light of this Jesus; the questions (and, from time to time, my hints at how these questions might be framed) must be worked at by those who can be bothered to pursue them.

It is my hope that there will be encouragement here for those who sometimes wonder where God is and why he seems to have gone missing. I also hope that this might be deeply irritating to the proud, the arrogant and those who see it as their calling in life to put God in a box and beat everybody else about the head and heart with it.

I am grateful to Linda, my wife, and Richard, Melanie and Andrew, my children, for giving me the space and encouragement to write. Much of this book was written at a time of great change for all of us. In May 2003, having only moved a couple of years previously from a parish in Leicestershire to South London (where I served as Archdeacon of Lambeth), I was appointed Bishop of Croydon in the Diocese of Southwark. This meant a further move and further adjustments in role, expectations and lifestyle. Following my consecration at St Paul's Cathedral, I flew to Austria for two weeks of rest, retreat and writing. I enjoyed the generous hospitality and company of the Türkis family and the Klaffenböck family in Traun. I am indebted to them for their friendship and fellowship.

Finally, I offer this reflection in the context of my life and ministry in the Diocese of Southwark and the Croydon Episcopal Area. I am privileged to serve here and am grateful to God for my colleagues, especially my fellow bishops under the leadership of Bishop Tom Butler. We are all very different, but pursue our journeys of discipleship with grace, generosity and respect. I think that is how it should be.

Chapter 1

FACING JERUSALEM

In one of the most powerful visual experiences of the early twenty-first century, the audience is invited to set out with Frodo Baggins and his friends from the settled tranquillity of the hobbits' Shire to journey to Mordor, the place of destiny and judgement. If the dangerous and eventful progress of the hobbits, elves, wizards and other assorted creatures was not enough, nine hours of film was more than some people could take. Frodo's regular temptations to give up the trip were mirrored by the audience's temptation to take refuge in popcorn or abandon the cinema to the people who would regard as sacrilege any criticism of Peter Jackson's *Lord of the Rings* trilogy. In this sense, the progress of the characters in the films reflects in some ways the experiences of those who found themselves enthralled by the films' narrative or simply bored by the idea of the rings in the first place.

There comes a point in any journey where the traveller knows that the point of no return has been reached. It might simply be that one has gone so far that there is no point in turning back now. Or it could be that there are strong psychological reasons why this particular journey must be completed, regardless of how far one has already gone. Indeed, that particular point can be reached even before the journey itself has begun. But it could also be, however, that one reaches a point both psychologically and physically at which a new view opens up before the eyes, and one is drawn towards the unknown future. Anyone who has walked in the Lake District of England knows this experience only too well: you tread the rocky path, looking at your feet and the way ahead, hearing your pulse throbbing in your ears as you trudge onwards and upwards until you turn the corner that reveals the valley and vista ahead of you while still allowing you to look behind and see whence you have come. And, setting your face towards the goal ahead, you feel the weakness of the knees as you begin to head downhill, your head up and eyes scanning the landscape before you. You know you are going to get there and it is just a matter of time; so you might as well enjoy the journey towards the inevitable destination.

What is true of the walker is also true of the traveller through life. There are times when the going is tough, or maybe just routine and unspectacular. But there sometimes comes a point when the future opens up and its possibilities or inevitabilities beckon. You still have the choice of going forward, staying put to savour the experience, or turning your back and returning. The problem, however, is that you can never go back exactly to where you began; the experiences that have brought you thus far mean that the world has changed: you have glimpsed new possibilities and have turned them down. Those who press on will do so with a mixture of motives: fatalism, recklessness, trepidation, adventure, joy or dread. The point is simply this: staying where you are for ever is not an option. You have to choose, and your choice will determine your future (or lack of it).

The pilgrim people of God

The people of God have always been called to travel. They have been invited or commanded to leave some things and places behind them and journey into the unknown – always travelling light and uncertain of their ultimate destination. Both metaphorically and really, this has always been the experience of those whom God has called his own – as a brief and selective excursion through the biblical narrative will demonstrate.

Adam and Eve

In the creation narratives of Genesis, human beings are called to leave the familiar social and family structures and cleave to another person. Adam is told that the responsibility for naming the animals is his – that God expects him to take responsibility and live with the consequences of his choices. After their encounter with the seduction of power, Adam and Eve are told to leave the Garden of Eden and enter a new world in which God will still care for them, but for which they will have to work and suffer. Their children also face choices which determine their own leavings (Abel of his life and Cain of the security of his previously known world and network of relationships).

Noah

Noah was just a good man with a good family and a vivid imagination. By heeding the prompting of God, he left behind his reputation (for sanity, among other things) and built a large boat in the middle of the desert. It is easy to read over this narrative with the benefit of hindsight and to miss the point that Noah had no hindsight and that his foresight was apparently off-beam. However, when the flood came and he was vindicated, there is no hint of 'I-told-you-so' self-righteousness; after all, he was leaving behind the world he knew and seeing his neighbours lose their lives. Noah did not leave his world and its routines behind in order simply to slip directly into a new world; rather, there was a very long period of nothingness and empty, fruitless waiting, with apparently no guarantees of a future. The journey probably looked different from within the ark to how it does from a cursory reading of the text.

Abram and Sarai

The narrative having opened up to the peoples of the world, Genesis 12 brings the focus back down to one man, one who will be the father of the nations although for most of his long life he has been completely ignorant of this calling. Abram is invited by God to leave Ur of the Chaldeans and go with his family 'to the land that I will show you'. He could have declined. An old man with an elderly wife, he could have suggested God would be better off with a younger man whose wife was still fertile. After all, both reason and experience would have been on his side, given that God's promise involved the childless couple in populating the world. The absurdity of this particular calling was not lost on Abram the retired, or on Sarai his barren wife, who laughed with derision when she was told what the future might hold. But they went anyway – and the rest is, as they say, history.

Moses

The people of Israel had been in captivity in Egypt for 400 years, and the oppression was getting heavier and harder to bear. All oppression is born of fear, and the

Pharaoh was no exception to this. It appears from the Old Testament narrative that there was no light at the end of this tunnel. But then a weak-willed murderer, compromised by a complicated ethnic identity and a bizarre and bewildering upbringing, is invited by God to confront the Emperor and threaten him with vengeance – not once, but seven times. All the excuses in the world (fear, pessimism, a more proficient brother, a stammer) won't let him shake off the calling that is his alone. To cut a long (and well-known) story short, Moses reluctantly does what he is told to do and leads his people to a liberation of sorts. But all this looked remote when Moses first came across a burning bush in the desert and thought that worship would simply involve removing his footwear and paying homage. In fact, a messy business involving blood, angels and deep waters opens the door to a scarcely believable new future in which freedom and new ways of living become possible.

The desert

However, the Bible does not encourage fantasy or illusion. This people is led out of captivity – not into a utopian theme-park of perpetual entertainment and eternal privilege, but into a desert where their mettle would be tested. It is not enough to be free from oppression; the future depends on the will to exercise freedom with responsibility for shaping the world as it ought to become. The liberated people of Israel want to leave responsibility behind with their oppressors, but the God who has created them, liberated them and called them will not be fobbed off with sentimentality. So, it is into the desert that they go, led by God him-self, and it is here, deprived of the imagined and illusory fruits of liberation, that they are faced with the inescapable questions of what sort of a people they are to be, what sort of a world they are prepared to shape, and at what cost this will come.

As the Asian theologian Kosuke Koyama has put it, they took forty years to learn one lesson: that you can't live by bread alone, but you need the word that proceeds from God himself if you are to be truly free and truly human. Simply to see freedom as a lack of oppression envisages a future and a world as full of opportunity as a vacuum is full of air. So the people of Israel journey through the desert, grumbling and mumbling, romanticising the past – yes, even the recent cruelly oppressive past – and seeking gods who will lead them on an easier path. The result is that many of them do not see the end of the people's journey to freedom in the land of promise, but die en route. Even Moses, the great hero of the story, dies having just glimpsed the goal of all his struggles, travels and travails. The journey followed by the individuals was an end in itself, not simply a means to an end which alone and of itself justified the journey in the first place.

Exile

It is perhaps not surprising that the journey of God's people continued to be bumpy. Called to be God's people for the sake of the world, these people saw their vocation instead as privilege. The warnings of the prophets (who saw reality more lucidly than ordinary mortals) were clear: recover the true nature of your calling as God's people, or the desert will once again be the place where your values and character undergo painful re-examination. Twice in 200 years, in the eighth century BC and the sixth century BC, the people lose their land, the guarantee of their identity and calling as God's people, and wonder if they have also lost their future. Indeed, how can they sing the songs of this Lord (creator, sustainer, sovereign ruler) in a strange land of exile where he appears to have been defeated, diminished and exposed as a fraud? The journey away from the security (psychological, political, national, economic) of 'home' is the means of their re-discovery of their true identity and vocation – to be the people of God, in the world but not of it, called to show God to this world which is God's, and to expend themselves in the fulfilling of this role. The eventual return of a remnant of this people does not permit them to indulge in the nostalgic recovery of past comforts. Rather, it forces them to remember who they truly are and to venture into a new future in the light of their past experience. They are not exactly successful.

Jesus

This calling of Israel is supremely fulfilled in Jesus, the builder from Nazareth in Galilee. Even in the womb of his young mother, he is on his travels as she and her husband ride to Bethlehem for the census. His birth leads to exile in the land that, for his people, characterises oppression and bondage: Egypt. Already, say the gospel-writers, the world and our expectations are being turned on their head: how can Egypt of all places ever be seen as a place of refuge? The world is not all it seems to be, and present reality does not represent all there is to be said on the matter. The answer will come with horror and surprise and will demand that we see differently and look through a different lens – one that ultimately will appear to be cross-shaped.

At the age of twelve, Jesus journeys to the metropolis, Jerusalem, where he engages in debate with the religious (and, therefore, political) teachers of his day. He more than holds his own, but returns to obscurity to continue his growth into adulthood. His calling is developing, and he has to wait until the time is right before he can go public. Indeed, his calling involved his growing up, his childhood and adolescence, his learning and questioning, his relationships and choices, his business and artistic life; it is ludicrous to suggest, as many do, that his calling was simply to die on a cross and be raised from the dead as if all that went before in his life was irrelevant to what and who the man became.

Clearly, the gospel-writers were not just filling in time when they carefully constructed their particular narratives. They put together the story of Jesus and his friends, fully aware of the implications of the structure they hung it on: the structures of the gospels are saying something to those who have the eyes to see and the ears to hear and who refuse to read the books in bite-sized fragments but, rather, see the narrative as a carefully worked whole. They constantly drop clues that intrigue and entice the reader to ask questions and read on.

When he eventually begins his public ministry, Jesus is first baptised in the Jordan by John the wild man of the desert. Emerging from the waters, a remarkable thing happens: Jesus sees and hears God's approval and affirmation and knows his life is about to change radically and irrevocably. But, instead of having a farewell party from his old life and home, he is led 'by the Spirit' into the desert to be tested. And here we hear echoes of another people at another time and in another place who were led by this same Spirit into a similar desert for the same purpose: Who are you?

What ultimately matters to you? What will characterise your kingdom? Are you entertaining an illusion – even a religious illusion – or facing the truth about yourself, your God, this world and your calling in it? His journey into this desert is no accident; it is a vital element of the experience and journey of all God's people at all times. Even God's Son is not exempted from the hunger, pain and tortured self-examination of it.

Following this experience, Jesus goes back to his home town of Nazareth. It might have been easier for him to preach his first sermon where people did not know him so well and where he could have got away with being more 'perfect' than those who had watched him grow up might wish to allow. But, no, Jesus returns to Nazareth and goes to the synagogue, where he reads the set lesson for the day (from Isaiah), sits down and preaches his inaugural sermon: 'Today,' he says with a completely straight face, 'this scripture has been fulfilled in your hearing'. The particular scripture involved here speaks of the chosen one of God being anointed to be the ultimate liberator and healer of God's people and, therefore, the world. To claim to be the subject of the divine text is almost blasphemous. And the sermon goes down so well with the people that they drag him out and try to throw him off a cliff. So much for affirmation from the people of God; so much for the people of God having ears to hear and eyes to see what doesn't appear to fit their pre-packaged theology and prejudiced biblical religiosity.

Jesus' friends

And this leads us to the point of this partial and selective reading of the story of God's pilgrim people, constantly being called to embark on a journey which leads them

into the unknown future with the sole certainty that
the God who calls them and beckons them to move out
will never leave them or abandon them – even though
this journey will lead them to their deaths. Jesus meets
strangers and invites them to leave what is familiar to
them and go with him on a journey, the end of which
they cannot possibly imagine. It will be a journey in
which they will be introduced to people and situations
that will make them uncomfortable. Their religious and
social presuppositions will be challenged to their roots.
Their world view will be threatened, disturbed and re-
shaped. They will find themselves completely out of
their depth and discover resources within themselves
which they would never have believed were there. They
will be invigorated, enthused, emboldened and excited
– but they will also be horrified, frightened, disillusioned
and humiliated.

However, all this will be done gently and in due
time. Jesus does not dump on them what they cannot
possibly bear. Rather, he leads them one step at a time,
allowing them to live a little longer with their theological
misconceptions and cultural prejudices, giving them
the space to witness, experience, try out for themselves,
and question all he does with them and for them. This
Jesus knows the clay with which he is working and
neither lumps it together in a blandly uniform pot, nor
discards what appears to be insignificant or hopeless;
indeed, he shapes the individually distinguished, yet
flawed, pieces that together make a full set.

Called to walk with Jesus

The new friends of Jesus probably had little or no idea
what Jesus had in mind when he asked them to go with
him. They surely had little understanding where all this

10

was going to lead them in the end. But, in asking them to accompany him, leaving behind some of the familiar things of life, he was inviting them to embody what had always been the calling of God's people: to travel light and be re-shaped along the way. It is a brave calling because it promises pain and loss. It is not for the faint-hearted or the romantic. It is only for those who know their need of God and his words and who are prepared to put one foot in front of the other in order to see where it will all lead. It is essentially only the curious who will go with Jesus, those who are not satisfied that 'this' is all there is, those who refuse to accept that the apparent way of the world is the only way the world can be.

The disciples of Jesus followed him with mixed motives and a variety of fantasies. But follow him they did. In one sense, that was all Jesus required of them: start the journey with me, and we'll see what happens along the way. He did not examine their theological soundness or doctrinal purity. He did not criticise their ethics or demand changes in their eschatology before they could come with him. He did not make sure that they would ultimately last the course before inviting them – they would have to choose for themselves whether or not they would go with him to the bitter end. Jesus let them be the people they were, with all their strengths and weaknesses, bringing with them the totality of their personality and character and bearing their own particular life story. They only had to be willing to walk – the rest would follow in due time.

Jerusalem, Jerusalem

For these friends of Jesus, as for the gospel-writers, the significance of one particular place in the story cannot be overstated. Jerusalem was at the heart of the religious establishment of Israel, the locus of all the people's nostalgia for a theocratic past glory and their hopes for a glorious ideal future in which their faith would be vindicated by the victory of their God over the unbelieving and idolatrous pagan nations. It was the place where God himself was present to the people, resident in the Holy of holies in the Temple, the guarantor of this people's vindication. It was the city where God's purposes had been and would be worked out in the sight of Israel's enemies. Roman imperial rule would not last for ever, and the occupying forces would be turfed out by the chosen one of God, thus ushering in the new age of God's almighty and ultimate reign. The history of this city would bear witness to the power of Israel's God exacting revenge for past humiliation and establishing a permanent throne from which he would preside over a new world order.

But Jerusalem was even more than this. It was the metropolis, the capital city of the nation, the locus of administrative order and political power. It may have been an obscure part of the great Roman Empire, but it was also the place where different peoples and economies met. When people spoke of Jerusalem, they evoked a concept that embraced political, economic, historical, religious and psychological power. The name itself represented and symbolised power, order and control. Here the rulers of the Empire were acknowledged and obeyed – albeit reluctantly – by the religious and political power-brokers of Judaism. When Rome was opposed, even in hopeless gestures of desperate rebellion, it was not the religious leaders who were leading from the front. Jerusalem was a place of despair, humiliation, hope and aspiration, a place of seething resentment alongside resentful compromise and collaboration with the Empire.

And it was to Jerusalem that Jesus and his friends ultimately set their faces. According to Luke's account, the pivotal point – the point of no return, as it were – came on the top of a mountain where three of Jesus' friends had an experience that they didn't fully understand. A little earlier, Peter had affirmed Jesus as the 'Messiah of God', the anointed one who would set Israel free. It is not clear just how Peter himself would have explained what he meant by this. But soon after, he went with James and John, and together they witnessed Jesus being shrouded in radiant light and conversing with two other men whom they took to be Moses and Elijah. Now, however, Jesus began to prepare them for the inevitable fate awaiting him. Resisting their desire to enshrine the religious experience of the moment, Jesus pulled no punches in telling them that they must now descend from the mountain and confront the principalities and powers on their own territory. 'He set his face to go to Jerusalem.'

The company Jesus keeps

Couldn't Jesus have done it differently? Couldn't his journey have been less suicidal and deliberately confrontational? And why did he have to take these poor innocents with him, knowing what would lie ahead for them and imagining the pain it would cause them and many others? Was it all really so inevitable, or could it have been avoided?

Jesus faced these questions at the outset of his public ministry when, after his baptism, he was led by the Spirit into the desert to be tested. What sort of kingdom was his to be? One that would play the world's power games by the world's rules? One in which material well-being and the satisfaction of personal need take precedence over a right way of living? One in which the image of spirituality matters more than the reality of what takes place in the hidden places of the body and soul? Or a kingdom in which God can be taken for granted and whose love can be abused – all for the sake of spiritual entertainment or titillation? Or one in which the painful path of integrity and faithfulness to God can be traded for power – a pain-free short-cut to glory in which the end bears no relation to the means?

The so-called 'temptations of Jesus' in the desert at the beginning of his public ministry were not the last time he was tested in this way. In Gethsemane, on the cross itself, and many times on the journey that preceded them, Jesus faced these awesome and awful choices. Whom would he heal, and where and when? Would he compromise his vision of God's character and kingdom in order to avoid pain and suffering for himself? Could not this cup pass him by? Was there no other way? And what if he had got it all wrong and this was all just a terrible waste, the delusion of a maniac? No, Jesus was not a superman impervious to the agony of doubt and the fear of pain; rather, he was fully aware of what this meant – for him, for his friends, for the world, and for God. And he set his face to go to Jerusalem.

Who goes there?

What is intriguing about all of this is just how risky the whole enterprise was. The friends of Jesus were not the sort of people every leader would want to have around them. Indeed, Jesus himself must have been free to choose not to walk the path laid out before him, but to seek an easier way to live and to die. The mere fact is that, if this is truly God's story and the story of God's people at a pivotal point in history, then we must be prepared to consider the fragile risk that God himself took in coming among us in this man, walking with these particular friends to these particular places, at this particular point in history in that particular part of the world. This book is an exploration of that story, of these people at that time and place; but, as we shall find, it is also peculiarly my story and our story together. If God still calls people to journey with him, we must begin with the journey he himself took with people like us; only then will we be able to hear the echoes of eternity resonating with our own experience and our own vocation to be God's people in and for God's world.

Chapter 2

PEOPLE LIKE US

There is a sense in which it is deeply regrettable that religious posterity has endowed people such as Peter and James and John with the title 'saint'. The fact that they are, in any sense of the word, saints is not in dispute. But the word itself now carries connotations of specialness and pure moral perfection that distance such people from the people we know ourselves to be and to be among. It is perhaps not insignificant that the stories of such people are less and less well known by our children and young people, or that the concept of sainthood has become faintly ridiculous – a term used to denote people who are not quite of the same world as the rest of us.

This is regrettable, because in the case of the characters whom we read about in the Bible, their humanity is only too evident. God seems only to deal with people who have feet of clay, motives as mixed and fickle as fool's gold, and relationship histories as colourful and patchy as a crocheted quilt. Yet somehow the saints who accompanied Jesus have become sanitised, bowdlerised and consigned to a rarefied unworldliness in the minds of many people today for whom they are a total irrelevance. Even in the Church, where their stories are read and preached about in disconnected fragments Sunday by Sunday, they have frequently become unreal phantasms of unattainable goodness. In the same way that tabloid newspapers distance the rest of us from the taint of any guilt or badness by proclaiming the Myra Hindleys of this world to be 'monsters', so 'saints' are disincarnated and disempowered by being reduced to the level of one-dimensional fantasy figures who clearly inhabited a different world from ours.

It is a tragedy of immense proportions that this has happened, because it demonstrates our inability to face reality and to live with the outrageous grace and mercy of God among us. All too often, the injunction of the preacher omits the details of those stories which complicate the convenient moral point being made. For example, Moses is not just the courageous and God-fearing leader and liberator of his people; he is also a redeemable murderer who suffers from near-terminal indecision. Abraham is not just the visionary and faithful follower of God's call for the world to be blessed through him; he also passes his wife off as his sister so that the local king can have his wicked way with her and not have the complication of dealing with a wronged husband. David is not just the great king of Israel and writer of wonderful poetry; he is also a liar, murderer and adulterer. Gideon might be a fantastic warrior, but he is also remarkably cruel to animals. Samson is a great hero of the people, but he is also morally brittle, led by his libido, strong of body and feeble of resolve. Jeremiah does what God tells him and says what God tells him to say; but he constantly whinges that he wishes he hadn't been born in the first place.

And so it is that when we come to the New Testament we get a few more surprises. In the long genealogies (ancestral histories) leading to the birth of Jesus, some rather bizarre people crop up whose names should not really be allowed to appear in polite company. We have already mentioned Abraham and David, but Jacob follows soon after; consider his relationship with his brother, his duplicity and selfish arrogance. Solomon had an interesting sex life and lost the plot towards the end of his life. And what of the women? Tamar had a colourful sexual history. Ruth wasn't even one of the chosen people of God – wrong ethnicity, wrong race, wrong creed. The wife of Uriah the Hittite (Bathsheba, though the genealogist does not name her) was an adulteress. Mary was pregnant before her marriage to an older man. Is Matthew trying to tell us something here?

Before proceeding any further, it is worth cross-referring this to the inclusion by the writer to the Hebrews of some dubious characters in the epic list of heroes and heroines of the faith. Rahab, a prostitute, appears in the same paragraph as the victorious and obedient conquerors of Jericho, honoured for her faith. The story of Rahab does not indicate that, after her heroic achievements, she changed her job.

This is not to encourage immorality or inconsistency in our living and behaving, but it is to make us face the fact that the Bible does not sanitise the people God chooses in the way many of us think it should. We are confronted by the anomaly that God chooses and uses ordinary people like the rest of us and often chooses people the rest of us would rather he didn't. (Pretend to be a Pharisee and listen to Jesus telling the parable of the Prodigal Son/Waiting Father/Elder Brother. Then re-write the story in relation to some of the highly charged theological and ethical debates facing the Church today.) The fact that they do marvellous things for God should neither disguise the fact that they remain flawed human beings nor expunge from their record the truth about their frailties and perversions. To do otherwise is simply to bowdlerise the Bible and pretend that neither we nor God can cope with reality in all its inconsistency.

A ragbag of saints and sinners

The point of all this is to pave the way for a consistent reading of the story of Jesus' journey to Jerusalem in the company of the particular characters whom he invited to join him. Saints they are, but saints only in the way the rest of us are: flawed, inconsistent, fearful, proud, weak, arrogant, ignorant and maybe even sometimes heroic. It is possible that, had the friends of Jesus had prior knowledge of who else was going to be walking with them, they might have declined the invitation. The mix of character, background and personality is rich, and, although for Jesus it might have had the hint of excitement experienced by anyone who has tried to arrange a conflict-free seating plan at a wedding reception, the potential for jealousy, competition and subversion was enormous. So, it is good that Jesus does the choosing and does not tell the invitees who else will be joining them, where they are ultimately going or what the whole journey is for.

Anyone who has gone on a pilgrimage will be familiar with this experience. Particularly if you go alone, you have no idea who will be accompanying you along the way. In fact, part of the purpose of a genuine pilgrimage is to throw you together with people whom you have never met before and with whom you might have nothing in common other than your participation in the journey. There is a perceptible randomness about the encounters you have. But you are compelled to engage in conversation with your fellow walkers, listening to their stories as well as sharing your own. Pilgrims begin to trust and to allow themselves to be exposed to the light of an erstwhile stranger's scrutiny. So, even though the pilgrim cannot necessarily choose her companions, she can learn to live with fellows she might not otherwise choose to know or like in ordinary life. The extraordinary context of the pilgrimage encourages, or maybe even demands, an engagement with people not like us. This sort of experience simply illustrates that it is easy to believe in the abstract conviction that God is love and loves everyone, but hard always to apply it in the particular when the irritating object of the conviction is there to see in all his spectacular and enfleshed uniqueness.

The friends of Jesus

It will help us to understand this more clearly if we look at some of the people whom Jesus invited to go with him on his three-year journey towards Jerusalem. Simon is not in church when Jesus meets him and asks him to walk up the beach with him; rather, he is at his place of work. He readily goes with Jesus (his middle name being 'impetuous') and finds himself in a very uncomfortable place. He frequently misunderstands what Jesus is saying and doing. He stands up in defence of Jesus, only to hear Jesus telling him off and apparently calling him 'Satan'. His own self-image is torn apart by his ultimate failure to stand by Jesus after the arrest in the Garden of Gethsemane, despite all the bold promises that he would protect his friend or stay with him to the bitter end. It is this same man who, on seeing Jesus walking on the water, jumps into the lake and promptly sinks.

So, how is it that Jesus chooses this man on whom to build his future new community? It would be interesting to know how the other disciples reacted upon hearing that from now on Jesus was going to call Simon by a new name (Peter, from the Greek *petros*, meaning rock ... 'Rocky'?) and make him the founder/leader of the Church. It is debatable whether Simon Peter would be allowed to become a minister, priest or bishop in the modern Church (of any denomination): he is impetuous, not the sharpest knife in the drawer, has illusions about his own character and does not know himself. It is good, then, that Jesus goes for potential rather than for the finished article.

James and John are brothers with the advantage or handicap (depending on how you view such things) of a pushy mother who harbours ambitions on their behalf. This ambition has rubbed off on the lads, colouring the way they hear and understand Jesus and what he is about. As good Jewish boys of the first century in the occupied territories of Palestine, they are longing for the destiny of their people to be fulfilled. They too are watching and waiting to see who the Messiah will be, the one who will liberate the people from Roman oppression and occupation and restore Jewish worship, order and pride once again. Power was perceived by them as the ability to lead the people to political, economic and military victory, thus vindicating the faith of the nation and restoring them to their correct status as God's most special people in the whole world.

It is no wonder, then, that they understand Jesus to be the likely liberator of the people, but can only conceive of this in the terms described above. They filter what Jesus says about freedom and forgiveness through the theological and historico-political lens of their prior experience and religious prejudice. Hence the misplaced family concern that, once Jesus has established his new post-revolutionary order, James and John will take pride of place at the head of the new cabinet, each sitting either side of Jesus in all his glory. They missed the fundamental point of all that Jesus was doing, saying and teaching. But Jesus kept them in the group of pilgrims and did not dismiss them because of their lack of comprehension, tactlessness or breathtaking arrogance.

And what about the women? Mary Magdalene appears to be of little repute. But she is one of the women who is not put off standing by Jesus as he dies on the public gallows, humiliated and tortured, his project apparently failed and his promises bleeding to death in the dirt of a brutal reality. It is she who goes to the tomb and becomes the first to meet the raised Christ in the garden. It is Mary who becomes the first evangelist, going to tell the others the good news of a rather surprising twist in the tail of the recent awful events.

Along with their brother Lazarus, Mary and Martha are friends of Jesus. But they are very different personalities, and they clearly have different priorities in life. When Jesus visits their home and enjoys their hospitality, one sits at his feet listening, learning and conversing with him; the other launches herself into hospitality mode and grows more bitter by the minute that she is doing all the work for Jesus the guest while her sister merely sits with him. The difference in their personalities is spelled out when Lazarus dies and the sisters send for Jesus. Jesus takes his time, and, before reaching their home, hears that Lazarus has died. One of the women (Martha) runs out to meet Jesus on the road and screams at him that if only he had come sooner Lazarus would still be alive. She accuses him of not caring, of being selfish, of getting his priorities wrong. Jesus absorbs the fierce blame and the accusations of lovelessness before engaging in some theological conversation with her. He does not despise her or justify himself. The other sister (Mary), meanwhile, is racked with grief, staying paralysed in her own home. When Jesus eventually gets there, she goes to him and makes the same accusation as that made by her more activist sister. But Jesus does not indulge in a repeat performance of the last conversation; rather, he simply weeps. Two sisters have different personalities, different ways of responding to life and death, two ways of grieving their loss, two ways of shouting at Jesus – and Jesus takes both on their own terms and responds appropriately to each. He does not rank them in order of theological consistency or psychological stability, but accepts and responds to both.

Surely the import of these pen portraits is obvious. Jesus chooses people who display all the failings and inconsistencies common to most of humanity. He does not force people to run before they can walk. He allows them to develop at their own pace, puts up with their misapprehensions and stubborn theological prejudices. He doesn't compare them and run some down at the expense of others who get the point more quickly. He doesn't rank them according to spirituality or gifts, but takes a long-term view of them, allowing them the freedom to be themselves as they accompany him on his journey to a cross and beyond.

The people who go with Jesus are not the people some of us would choose to lead our churches and become accredited evangelists. They are too messy. They fail too often. They are inconsistent. Perhaps they are too human for us. But they are the people whom Jesus called anyway. Some will argue that this does not take account of what happens to the disciples later, particularly after Pentecost. However, the onus is on them to look at post-Pentecost Peter (for example) and explain his altercation with Paul, the conversion in his eating habits and his difficulty in making decisions in the Church. His personality has not changed: he is still Peter, and there will still be those who think his name a mistake in character description. But Jesus chose Peter, inspired and transformed him ... while still letting him be Peter. Perhaps the difference between the pre-crucifixion and the post-Pentecostal Peter is to be found in the account that comes between the two when the post-resurrection Jesus once again meets him back at his place of work, the beach. Here he once again invites Peter to go for a walk with him and asks him three times if he loves him. Prior to Calvary, three times Peter had denied knowing Jesus; three times Jesus allows Peter to re-affirm his love after the resurrection. The difference is simply that Peter has lost all the illusions he once held about himself and his own self-sufficiency. Peter does not cease to be Peter (with all that that means and implies); but humility makes all the difference in following Jesus and leading a church.

Mixing with the wrong people

The synoptic gospels have become so familiar to some Christians that the power of their challenge has become diminished. It is as if we have become so used to hearing the joke that the punchline has either got lost or seems no longer to be funny. Early readers of the books would probably have got the point.

According to Matthew, after the birth of Jesus in Bethlehem he was visited by shepherds (rough working men of low social class who couldn't be regular church-goers because of the demands of their work) and Magi (astrologers from a foreign country) – in other words, two sets of outsiders whom the religious leaders, the guardians of the truth, would not have regarded as members of God's acceptable community. To add insult to injury, Jesus and his parents then have to find refuge and salvation from that same community in a pagan country notable for its history of oppression and persecution of God's people. The symbolism is striking and, presumably, neither accidental nor coincidental.

Having begun his public ministry, Jesus then immediately goes around healing the sick, the diseased, cripples, the mentally ill and demonically demented people. In other words, he goes straight to the people who find no place in the religious heart of the nation or community. These are people who have become an embarrassment, surely ill because of the sins of themselves or their parents. These are the people who contribute nothing to society, but simply take from it (in begging, for instance). Yet, when Jesus proclaims the coming of the kingdom and the need for a change of ways of seeing and being, it is to these people that he goes. His kingdom is not the same as that experienced or imagined by the people; and it is not quite what the Messiah was expected to bring in, either.

Read the all-action beginning of Mark's gospel, and the same observation can be made. Those who think they are acceptable to God can look after themselves. But Jesus, this Jesus whom we now worship as Lord and Saviour, breaks all the rules and the taboos and brings healing to those who need it but don't (according to religious wisdom) deserve it. Messy people find an embrace in the arms of Jesus and discover that God is on their side. Meanwhile, the religious people just get more irritated with Jesus' wrong-headed priorities. The guardians of doctrinal purity and legalistic orthodoxy – despite using the language – always did find grace a problem: instead of it being a gift to be received in transforming experience, they turn it into a dogma by which to judge who is acceptable to God and, by implication, to the community of 'the chosen'.

The gospels are full of shocking surprises to those who are alert enough to recognise them. Those of no account in the political and religious context of his time found in Jesus of Nazareth that God knows them by their real name and loves them. These, the sad losers of a society that prided itself on knowing who was 'in' and who was 'out', were the very people to find in Jesus' touch their body and spirit healed, their dignity restored and their future opened up for them once again. In Jesus' words they were shocked to hear their name spoken, their place guaranteed and their eyes opened. When Jesus told the parable of the sheep and the goats to bewildered people who kept finding their world view being shaken, he knew that it would be offensive to some and incredible good news to others. For, in this story, it is those who take God for granted, who 'put the law of God above the God of the law', who find themselves having missed the point and lost their place – for them the gospel of Jesus was not very good news after all. And it was those who had not calculated with God and not played religious games with him who found themselves included in the kingdom of God's new order – for them this was very good, but rather startling and confusing news. It might just be significant that this point has been missed or lost by those who claim to be closest to God today, especially those who will exclude even other friends of Jesus simply because they cannot agree on every last word of a particular statement of faith or code of conduct.

Selection criteria

This brief look at some of the people whom Jesus invited to come with him and some of the people whom they met along the way demonstrates just how dangerous Jesus is to those who think discipleship is about getting their doctrine word-perfect or their religious devotions complete. Both of these may be laudable, but they are to be a response to the gracious goodness of an outrageously generous God who seems to get upset only with those who complacently exclude from the community of faith those who can't tick all the boxes that the guardians of that faith have decided must be ticked. Indeed, Jesus is scandalous in his generosity and lack of orthodoxy in whom he chose to be his friends and whom he chose to heal.

All of these people responded to Jesus in a way that meant letting go and leaving behind some elements of their life and make-up if they were to accompany Jesus on his journey. The only thing required of them was a willingness to set out on foot. For Peter, it meant taking time out of his work. For blind Bartimaeus, it meant getting his sight back but at the same time losing his life of passive begging and taking responsibility again as a fully responsible and contributing member of society. For the leper and other outcasts, it meant leaving behind their narrow horizons and the stigma of disease and becoming human again. For the woman of no name who was the object of mockery in her village, it meant receiving a name, a place in the community and all that comes with knowing that God had restored her. To respond to Jesus meant change in body, mind and spirit.

It seems that Jesus was painting on a canvas wider than even his close friends could see. He saw the potential of those whom he met and called. He would not be limited by the restrictions and formulaic orthodoxies of his cultural heritage, but confounded the same by seeing through them to the end for which they were supposed to be the means, namely the kingdom of God and its priorities in the mind and affections of God.

This is summed up in a pithy outburst by Jesus after having been questioned by the followers of John the Baptist. John is in prison and sends his friends to ask Jesus if he is really and truly the Messiah or just another forerunner. Jesus, invoking the 'proofs' offered by the Old Testament prophet Isaiah, tells them to make up their own minds on the basis of what they can see with their own eyes: 'the blind receive their sight, the lame walk, the lepers are cleansed, the deaf hear, the dead are raised, and the poor have good news brought to them'. But he then goes on to say that people keep looking in the wrong place for the Messiah. They expect a royal and military leader but, instead, get a man who mixes with poor people and seems to have read the wrong script for the messianic role. His damning indictment concludes with this ironic complaint: 'But to what will I compare this generation? It is like children sitting in the market places and calling to one another, "We played the flute for you, and you did not dance; we wailed, and you did not mourn". For John came neither eating nor drinking, and they say, "He has a demon"; the Son of Man came eating and drinking, and they say, "Look, a glutton and a drunkard, a friend of tax-collectors and sinners!" Yet wisdom is vindicated by her deeds.'

And we might be tempted to add, in the context of the contemporary Church, *plus ça change*. You just can't win. John abstains in order to be prophetic, and the clergy think he is mad; Jesus indulges, and they write him off as a windbag. The irony is that what was clearly intended to be a sarcastic put-down by the religious rulers was taken by Jesus to be a compliment: he was the friend of sinners and, by implication, not the friend of the arrogant, the self-righteous or the complacent. But this wasn't a case of Jesus being bigoted about smug people; it was simply that some people danced to his tune and others didn't. Those who knew their need were able to hear the melody and respond, either in grief or in joy. But some were deaf to it and merely condemned by ridicule what they could not immediately comprehend.

Jesus' pilgrim people

Jesus set his face to go to Jerusalem, and he took with him a group of companions who clearly, and despite his warnings, did not understand what lay ahead. Their world view still did not allow space for what Jesus was about to endure and could not register the theological, psychological or social significance of the events about to unfold. They would be caught up into something that would shock and terrify them and leave their world of expectations in bloody tatters in a lonely tomb. But Jesus, as always, paints on a larger canvas and takes a long-term view of his friends. One day, the penny will drop and they will put the pieces of their experiences and his words together, and it will begin to make sense. It will revolutionise and offend all they have hitherto held to be true about God, the world and themselves; yet it will also bring them back to where their faith was intended to lead them in the first place: to a creator God who is outrageously generous and scandalously forgiving of this ragbag of saints and sinners whose sole virtue is to have been themselves and lost their illusions. And if this were true for them, it must surely be true for the world.

Chapter 3

BETRAYAL

There never was a golden age of the Church. From the beginning, the *ekklesia* of God's people was a ragbag of saints and sinners, people who emphasised their own theological preferences over against those of other Christians, people who damned the sins of their fellow believers while remaining blind to their own. Their faith and religious practice were influenced by the cultural norms of their particular historical and social context. Therefore, when people remark (usually dismissively in avoiding taking responsibility for being and shaping the Church of today) that if only we could get back to the simplicity of the early Church everything would be fine, it is tempting to ask whether they have in mind any particular early Church: Corinth with its interesting sexual dynamics, Galatia with its problems over circumcision (what one has to go through to become a Christian and a member of the Church), or Philippi with its first- and second-class believers (depending on whether they had Roman citizenship or not)? The first Christians were no different from today's Christians in not being of a single mind on every issue; although circumcision is not often demanded of new converts today, matters of sexuality do not find a simple and united response from all Christian churches everywhere on the planet. To wish it could be different or to romanticise history is merely a form of escapism that betrays an unwillingness to face the challenges of today, a failure to take responsibility for taking risky decisions and living with the consequences.

It is quite remarkable that this should be in any way remarkable. A reading of the Bible (any of it) would show us that God's people are a mess and always have been. This is not a state of affairs that should be romanticised or defended, but it must be recognised and ought to produce in all believers a certain humility in their relations with each other and the world which they are called to serve. Indeed, the friends of Jesus are instructive for us if we only have the eyes to see and the ears to hear what they have to say to us about the realities of discipleship.

Supper and symbols

When Jesus entered Jerusalem for the final time, he did so knowing that the place was buzzing with anticipation. Was now the time when God would do the business for his people? Passover is the feast at which Jews recall and re-live the events of their liberation from Egypt in the Exodus. It foreshadows for them the action of God that they now await with longing and passion. Once again, in this anticipated new exodus, he will come and deliver them from their captivity, thus bringing to an end the 'exile' they have been enduring at the hands of the Romans and other oppressors. The friends of Jesus would have been caught up in this speculation and yearning, too – which makes it all the more ironic and dramatic that they cannot see and do not understand what is being played out among them and before their very eyes.

As they eat and drink the elements of this meal, bread and wine among them, Jesus re-symbolises what to good Jews represented the most powerful language of hope and the fulfilment of God's promises. While their minds reflect on the exodus of Moses, a freedom bought with the price of blood and by the singular activity of God (they could not save themselves), Jesus points to a new exodus for which they do not yet have a conceptual framework. When he said, 'Take, eat, this is my body which is given for you', did they laugh? Or did they sit in silence, just wondering what he was on about this time? Or did they think he was having delusions of messianic identity which he had somehow perverted? Or did they just think it was one more enigmatic contribution from their enigmatic and charismatic leader/rabbi? The gospel-writers do not tell us.

What we do know, however, is that what followed was unmistakably clear. According to John, Jesus, the teacher and rabbi, takes himself away from the table, puts a towel around his waist, kneels at the feet of his bewildered companions and begins to wash their feet. Their protests do not fall on deaf ears, but rather on ears that understand all too well the power structures of this world. The master does not wash the feet of the servant; it must be the other way round. How is order to be maintained in society if the conventions of rank and place are dismantled or subverted? What Jesus is doing is both threatening and offensive, thus provoking in Peter at least a strong reaction of disgust. But in this action, which is all of a piece with the words that have preceded and will succeed it, Jesus introduces the disciples to his new kingdom and the upside-down values that apply there. In other words, where Jesus is, different rules will apply and a different life will be lived, one characterised by mutual service and sacrifice, one in which rank and status have no place in terms of human value, one in which leadership is essentially and primarily diaconal.

So it is that a meal with which all these people are familiar is transformed into a shared experience of revolution, even if most of the participants still have little or no idea what is going on. As with most things in life, it is only with hindsight that we put the threads together and recognise what has been happening. Only then it is usually too late to capture the moment, and we find ourselves, like Peter, James and John upon the Mount of Transfiguration, not permitted by God to enshrine the experience, but told to move on to whatever is coming to us next.

The most surprising feature of this meal, however, is easy to overlook. It is simply this: Jesus does not kneel at the feet of people who have grasped his point and been converted to his new kingdom's ways of seeing, thinking and living; rather, he kneels at the feet of the one who will betray him for money; the one who, despite statements of undying loyalty, will shortly deny even knowing Jesus; the ones who cannot see beyond the status and power which they wish to achieve after the liberation;the ones who are silent, and those for whom the power and significance of this event passes by in a mist of incomprehension. Jesus washes the feet of *these* people, not those of the grateful and the theologically sound. It is a scandal and ought to be deeply embarrassing even to us who read of it 2,000 years later. It is the scandal of grace.

Competing melodies

Any attempt to follow the friends of Jesus on their journey to Jerusalem with him will make us realise the dilemma of discipleship. We might long to be consistent and to hear 'the trumpet sound a clear note' on every theological issue imaginable. But it is not, and never has been, possible for this to happen conclusively and definitively. It is the human lot – even for Christians – to live in a world in which different melodies are being played, demanding that we choose which one to listen to. But this task is not easy. There will be times when one melody dominates and the other can be left in the background of our consciousness where it need not perturb us. But then, when the balance is disturbed (by circumstance or emotion), the conflict between the tunes produces an enervating cacophony which cries out for resolution. We would like to switch one melody off at source, but find that this is not possible; it simply goes with the territory of being alive in a dynamic and evolving world that the conflicting lines of music will continue to compete. The business of life is to do with the never-ending attempt to listen to the sound of the best tune and follow the line of the music with all the integrity and discipline we can bring to the task. Try listening to the Rolling Stones' *Sticky Fingers* and Mozart's *Requiem* at the same time, and you will get the point.

This illustrates the experience of Jesus' friends, both then and now. The world is a complicated place and full of noise. Different voices clamour for our attention, claiming to offer wisdom for living but coming from different mouths and leading to diverse (and often incompatible) conclusions in ethics and values. For the pilgrims on the way to Jerusalem with their intriguing rabbi, this generated interesting and infuriating conflicts. The norms and assumptions underlying contemporary religious understandings of the world were constantly being challenged and subverted by what Jesus said and did. It is probable that, had Peter and his friends fully grasped what Jesus was on about, they would have left him quickly and returned to the routine of normal life.

Take God, for instance. God loves those who obey Torah, the law which he had personally given to Moses centuries before. This was the immutable code of ethics and relationships for the people, and it was rooted in a conviction that this was the last word in God's word to his people. If, therefore, one's primary aim in life is to obey the law as closely to the letter as possible, what do you do when someone comes along who assumes the mantle of Moses and re-interprets that same law in a new way? How do you cope with one who calls into question the very basis on which you have lived your life and done your ethics? Does it not seem just a tad arrogant for Jesus to imply that he knows the mind of God better than Moses (who, according to the scriptures, met God face to face on the mountain) and is the only one to understand that the people have been missing the point for generations?

For that is the situation for the first disciples and their compatriots. Jesus seemed to be saying that they had mistaken the means for the ends and that the law and its regulations were intended to bring people into a right relationship with God, other people and the created order itself. Instead, he said, fulfilment of the law had become the end of the matter. Obey the law, and God will be pleased – a sort of cosmic test for individual and communal human beings. Jesus, however, saw it differently and aimed to remind people of the rock whence they had been hewn, recalling them to embrace the point of the law anyway, which was to experience the grace and love of God for his whole creation and live in grateful response to it.

Jesus heals a crippled woman on the Sabbath. The local religious enthusiasts are furious with him. Does he not know that what he has done counts as 'work' and that working on the Sabbath is contrary to God's will and declared law? Is he being deliberately obtuse and looking for trouble? Why couldn't he heal the woman on a Tuesday or a Thursday or even late afternoon on a Friday before sunset? They have missed the point that God's healing is something to be celebrated, that this is precisely what the Sabbath was all about in the first place and that, anyway, the Sabbath was made for the benefit of people and not the other way around. The Sabbath was created to allow people to be free from the compulsion of work for one day in order that they should recall their vocation to be children of a creator God of grace and mercy. But, as is clear from this and many other events recorded in the gospels, the people saw the Sabbath as an end, not as a means. From this, it would appear that it is possible to enshrine the symbol and lose sight of what the symbol represents or points to; a bit like arguing in church about the choice of hymns or songs and forgetting for whom and why we sing them in the first place.

It would be intriguing to know what the disciples were thinking when Jesus told his parables. For example, what reaction did their faces betray when he was relating the story of a young man who told his father he wished he were dead and could he please have his share of the inheritance now? The father lets him go, knowing that the only way he can learn is by making his own mistakes. Taking a long-term view of things, he cashes in his son's share of the family's assets and watches him go off to spend it. Some time later, years perhaps, the son has exhausted the money and himself and sees no future except to return to his father and seek employment, which at least would allow him to live and give him a roof over his head. Having been reduced to an obscene level of poverty during a famine and having squandered his fortune and his friends, the wayward son returns. He works out his story and how he will beg of his father to receive him back, not as a son but as a hired worker. However, the father has been looking out for him, constantly living in contradiction to his experience and in hope of a miracle, and runs out to meet his errant son; he breaks all conventions by lifting his skirt and running. His son cannot even get the words out of his mouth before his father is embracing him and welcoming him home.

So far, the story has already caused scandal. First, any respectable father who has brought his son up properly and respectfully would not find himself in this position anyway; so, what sort of a father was he to raise a son so badly? Second, his son's arrogant and cruel demand should have been met with punishment; it should certainly have led to the son being disowned and disinherited by his father. Where is this father's self-respect? Third, he should wait for the son to demonstrate his abject apologies before even opening his own mouth or touching the wastrel; is he a glutton for humiliation? Fourth, the father should put his own dignity and moral status first and not allow them to be debased by this unreliable and disgraceful offspring; so why does he take him back in any capacity?

Then, as if this were not enough, Jesus pushes the story towards breaking point. Justice cries out on behalf of the young man's elder brother who has stayed with his father, working the estates and being a good boy. He is outraged by his father's generosity towards his profligate brother – and those listening to the story would have shared in his indignation. The father's behaviour is not only outrageous by the cultural standards of his day and place, but it is fundamentally immoral. Where is justice in all this? And punishment? What is the world coming to when justice is ignored and the sinner welcomed home with extravagance and joy?

It is clear from this story that the religious authorities of Jesus' time were the target of this stinging rebuke. But it would still be instructive to know what the disciples made of it. The Hebrew scriptures are littered with examples of the staggering generosity of God, a generosity that outweighs even justice itself. It is not unjust towards anyone – the elder son has been paid, fed and housed and will one day inherit the estate – but it is absurdly generous towards those who deserve only justice. This is the message of Jonah, Hosea, Amos and the prophets. It is the thread that runs through much of Jesus' teaching. And it is the single most important element in his behaviour towards those whom he met and healed and with whom he shared his life and time and food. But, for the disciples as well as for the Pharisees, it didn't fit the picture that their world view had them expect. It would take time to sink in ... if it weren't to be immediately rejected as foolish.

Judas

Understanding is always conditioned by context and culture, and it takes humility to live with provisionality in belief and behaviour. The disciples still had not grasped the import of Jesus' parables even when he shared his last supper with them and spoke in words of one syllable (metaphorically, of course) about what he and his imminent end was all about. It is perhaps here that the clash of expectations and understandings creates a radical disharmony in which the only way through seems to be to force Jesus to name his tune and make it fit in with the other melody. It is Judas who seeks a resolution to this conflict – and he does so by an act of what might be called 'loyal betrayal'.

The paradox for Judas is that he is a good man with noble values who longs to see the kingdom come and God's will be done on earth as in heaven. He is the keeper of the group's purse, and he is both moved and motivated by the plight of the poor of his land. He is as much against the rulers of his own people as he is against the Roman imperial occupying forces. He also has been waiting for the messianic liberation, and he thinks Jesus might be the man. But Jesus has an infuriating habit of not sticking to the messianic script as it was interpreted by Judas. He was being too slow in bringing in the revolution, and he was possibly being terribly talkative and intriguing when Judas was looking for decisive action. Surely, he thinks, enough is enough; if Jesus is put in a position of vulnerability, he will have no option but to come out fighting. So, he agrees to betray him to the religious powers in order to see what will happen.

Now it is not clear exactly what was going on in Judas' mind at this time, but we can glean a certain amount from the context and from what we know of the sort of profile people like Judas had. Whatever the truth about the details of his psychological make-up and the rationale for his behaviour, we can infer that there was some internal conflict for him. He was trying and wanting to harmonise what ultimately cannot and will not be harmonised: the way of the world and the way of Jesus. Despite all this, however, it is not clear just what his betrayal of Jesus represents. It is perfectly possible that his motives were good and his passion laudable, but his understanding was limited and his method unfortunate. No wonder he was devastated to the point of suicide when the plot turned an unexpected corner and he realised he had made a catastrophic error from which there could be no escape. It is only idle speculation, but we might wonder what conversation he might have had after the resurrection as he walked up the beach with Jesus.

Who betrays whom?

In the messy world of human life and politics, it is not always clear who is betraying whom. Judas evidently felt betrayed by Jesus; all the hopes of liberation seemed to be coming to nothing, and his hopes and longings were once again being bitterly disappointed. He could not see through to the far more radical liberation that Jesus was achieving in the new exodus: the ending of Israel's long exile, the forgiveness of sins and the opening of a new age – one in which grace and mercy make even justice seem inadequate for those who hold no illusions about their own need. Judas was an activist who wanted to make history and to force fundamental change in the social order right here and now. Not for him the lesson of Israel's long history that God will not have his hand forced and will not be rushed.

If there is any characteristic of God in the scriptures that is totally consistent throughout Israel's story, it is his immoveable resolve to wait for the *kairos*, the right time. Israel spent 400 years in Egypt before being liberated, only then to see generations die in a forty-year sojourn in the desert before entering the Promised Land. Centuries later, the prophets came and recalled the people back to their 'servant' status in the world, warning that failure to respond would inevitably lead to historical processes of political weakness, economic collapse and military occupation. The ensuing exiles (with their loss of land and the symbols of God's favour and presence) would work their course, and an end would only come at the right time. Several hundred years elapsed between the return to the land and the advent of John the Baptist (reminiscent of Elijah, that great and faithful man of God from those dark days centuries ago) and Jesus.

Jesus was born as a vulnerable human being and found his life in danger from the beginning. Exiled and hunted, he eventually grew up in a northern village in an obscure part of the Middle East. His childhood and adolescence were fairly unremarkable (or, at least, they are barely remarked upon by the gospel-writers), and it was not until he was thirty years old that his public ministry began. God will not be rushed. God takes a long-term view of things and people.

Learning to wait

Having set his face to go to Jerusalem, Jesus knew that his time was coming to an end. Judas couldn't wait for him. His betrayal was symbolic of those who suffer at the hands of those who use power to achieve a short-term goal even at the expense of any long-term solution. Betrayal is an unavoidable part of the experience of a God who makes himself vulnerable to human beings and the complexities and contradictions in their passions and commitments. In Psalm 22, the poet evokes the agonised cry of one who has been forsaken; Jesus is not surprised by his own delivery into the hands of his accusers and soon-to-be torturers. It is part of the cost of being grasped by the good news of God's kingdom in a world where people are either slow to grasp it or find it so threatening that they must expunge all evidence and threat of it.

God's hand cannot be forced – even by people who pray passionately and with conviction for what they assume God must inevitably favour anyway. Some will pray and feel betrayed by a God who doesn't do what the script has told us he must do – heal the sick child, for example. And some will be so scandalised by God's apparent inactivity that they will subsequently betray him to a world that does not find grace or generosity easy to deal with. But, as is always the case in the experience of Jesus and his friends, there is an alternative: that we learn to wait and open ourselves to the possibility that our script might need to be read differently – through different eyes, as it were. It will mean accepting that we might not have apprehended the whole truth of the gospel and might need to place ourselves with the generous wronged father, the undeserving returning son, the cynical and hurt elder brother ... or Judas in his sense of betrayal that gives birth to the betrayal of the one who had knelt at his feet and served him as a slave.

Jesus knew what he was doing and to whom he was doing it when he knelt before Judas. Those who journey with Jesus today must revisit that place and that action regularly. Unless we learn from and behave like Jesus before Judas, we make a mockery of the kingdom and negate the gospel itself. We may need to comprehend – even be sympathetic to – those who, because of their own experience of life, themselves feel betrayed by God or the world. Even if they behave madly or badly, trying to force God's hand or using their perceived 'victimhood' as a justification for all sorts of appalling words or actions, we may still need to kneel at the feet of betrayers – not because God will force them by our humility to see more clearly, but simply because Jesus sees such humility as an end in itself, even if the betrayer later (and single-handedly) opts out of the possibility of restoration and reconciliation.

The gospels are unequivocal in their depiction of Jesus' journey through life to a cross at Calvary in the company of such messed-up people: their judgement is captured in that scene in which Jesus kneels at the feet of his betrayer and serves him – an act of supreme love and dignity, not the misguided act of an over-optimistic and deluded romanticist. Generosity and grace colour the kingdom of which the church, the body of Christ, is supposed to be the evidence. Which means ... ?

Chapter 4

DENIAL

It is possible that Judas was a fantasist. If so, he is not alone among humanity. He might have wanted to see the kingdom come in a particular way and might have been disappointed by Jesus' unwillingness to act according to the political and ideological script that Judas felt he should have been following. But if Judas was fostering an illusion of liberation that, had it been realised, would have led to other injustices and cycles of ongoing violence and resentment, it is another of Jesus' chosen people who struggles to face reality, especially the truth about himself: Simon, who was to be re-named Peter, the Rock. Even the name is ironic, given the nature and story of this man. He may have been rock-like in his image of his own strength and integrity, but when the chips were down he was simply petrified.

It appears to be an essential feature of human individuals and their communities that we tell our stories in such ways as to boost our own status by diminishing that of others. This can be seen at all sorts of levels of human society, intercourse and historiography. Facts that do not fit the story which we wish to be heard are simply filtered out; it is not exactly that we always wish to hide them, we simply don't see their continuing relevance to the particular story we are telling. How we tell our stories, however, determines our identity and, therefore, our significance. So, what is included in or excluded from the stories we tell of ourselves or our communities or nations matters a great deal. And sometimes it is just easier to leave some facts out and place them somewhere less embarrassing to the integrity of our narrative. It might help to illustrate this briefly, not in order to give a definitive account of any specific people, but merely to illustrate the essential point.

The Armenian genocide

In 1915, the Turkish government embarked on a systematic elimination of Armenian people, places and history. The Armenians, especially those who are survivors of the atrocity, have to fight even now to get the world to face the truth of what happened to them and their families. Successive Turkish governments have been totally consistent in two respects: first, they have systematically covered up what happened, even to the extent of removing archaeological remains of villages and churches as if to prove they never existed in the first place; second, they still deny that the genocide ever took place. Not only can there be no justice for the Armenian descendants of those who suffered and died; there can be no reconciliation or 'closure' on the part of the victims because of the denial of the perpetrators. This genocide is a weeping wound that cries out primarily for recognition, let alone healing. The tragedy is further exacerbated by the unwillingness of other countries (especially western ones) to compel Turkey to address its own history properly. We live in a world in which the proclaimed abuse of human rights in one country deserves to bring forth the wrath of military invasion, while that in other countries can be ignored where political or military expediency dictates this to be the best course.

Iraq

The political justification in the USA and the UK for the military onslaught against Iraq in 2003 was twofold: first, Saddam Hussein runs a regime that has quickly deployable weapons of mass destruction and is a threat to other Middle Eastern and western countries; second, Saddam Hussein is a tyrant who terrorises his people, and this presents the west with a moral imperative to deliver the poor Iraqi people from their suffering. Both elements used the language of freedom, democracy and morality to argue for what many people around the world regarded as a cynical and economically driven move against the Iraqi state.

The main reason for this cynicism was the fact that Saddam was reinforced and financed by western countries such as the USA and the UK during the 1980s, when it was convenient to bolster the opposition against the enemy of the day, Iran. When Saddam was gassing the Kurds, persecuting the Shias and torturing and executing his opponents at will, the west turned a blind eye. The short-termism of the politics of pragmatism made concerns about tyranny and irresponsible ownership or development of weapons of mass destruction irrelevant and inappropriate. After all, Saddam was *our* tyrant and apparently on our side. If it had not been for some politicians, the churches and some journalists constantly reminding people of these uncomfortable facts, the public reading of history in 2003 would have been remarkably selective. Denial of western complicity in the grooming of Saddam was dangerous enough, but for it to be consciously and deliberately done with the language of truth, morality and ethical imperatives was positively wicked. The

49

irony was not lost on anyone except those responsible for the public utterances of governments. Yet it was encouraging that ordinary people were not prepared to collude in this act of official denial. (This is not to deny the rightness or wrongness of the case for war, but merely to question the apparently selective official omission of historical facts in the presentation of that case.)

It could be argued that these two examples are easy and extreme targets. But this would be to miss the point that they are simply illustrative of how readings of history are often shaped or re-shaped in order to justify a particular ideological commitment. The museum housed underneath the Indonesian national monument in Jakarta has a display of ships sailing from Sumatra to Java several thousand years ago; the interesting feature, however, is that they bear the flag of late twentieth-century Indonesia. The entire exhibition was designed to give historical legitimacy to the then current (Soeharto) regime. Given that no reading of history can be complete, objective and untainted by motivated selectivity, there is a massive difference between a deliberate denial of certain histories and a denial that is unconscious or born of ignorance of its relevance. Nevertheless, depending on where one stands in relation to the history being recorded and the story being told, the fact of denial may have the same effect: frustration, anger and the loss of trust. And from these bitter roots grows a dangerous cynicism.

A cursory glance at the Palestinian intifada (a dangerous thing to do) provides a tortured and immensely sad example of what happens when the legitimacy of a people's story and history is denied. The bitter and cruel language that characterises relations between Israel and the Palestinians, made concrete by the building of walls and fences, arises partly from the inability or unwillingness of one people to acknowledge the place and story of the other. To do so would be to legitimise the claims that might arise from that experience or history. If Israelis were to acknowledge the Palestinian grievance arising from callous dispossession of land and homes – the denial of their nationhood, dignity, history and personhood – they would have to accept the validity of the grievance and the legitimacy of their being. To do so, however, would be too costly politically, so the grievance is denied and the past ignored. Of course, this is also the case that might be put against the Palestinians by the Israelis, and they will argue for ever about when 'history' in the so-called Holy Land actually began. But what this demonstrates is that the denial of a people's story is a denial of their being; the question of 'rights' is secondary to the need to be heard and to have one's story acknowledged and its implications faced. The present and the future only make sense when seen in the context of the past. The novelist Laurens van der Post once observed that he who has no story to tell has no life to live. He was right.

Story and identity

It is important to recognise that, even though religion and religious commitment can never be purely individual, but always involve subjects in community, communities are made up of subjects who have their individual personal histories, perspectives and commitments. Indeed, part of what gives a person identity and a place in the world is the identification of his own story with that of the community or communities to which he belongs. While life is simple and one belongs to only one or two communities (extended family and work, for example), this may present few problems and little need to question one's own place or story. However, problems can arise when life becomes more complicated (as in modern mobile society), when one belongs to a variety of communities which may or may not have any connection with each other. To put it crudely, if you live in a single fairly static (or self-contained) society in which you live, work, socialise and die, life will be considerably more simple, and the story which defines that community may be re-told and owned with little question; the mere existence of the community validates the truth and integrity of the story. If, on the other hand, you have lived in six different places and communities before you leave school, meeting new and diverse people and cultures, all telling different stories in different languages and using diverse criteria for recognising the validity of their own history, then life and identity become somewhat more complicated.

So, the story and identity of any individual is inextricably intertwined with the story or stories of the community or communities in which he or she has grown and been nurtured and with which he or she has identified. And so it is with Peter, friend of Jesus, the rock who melted when the heat was on.

The rock from which Peter was hewn

We have already seen how the melody of first-century Jewish messianic expectation and the melody of Jesus' kingdom seemed to clash unharmoniously. Those whose history and faith told them that God would once again deliver them from captivity and vindicate both himself and them before the eyes of the world found themselves threatened by the approach of Jesus who seemed messianic in parts but seemed to have departed from the received score, improvising melodies that didn't sound quite right – a bit like playing jazz in a concert of Mozart concertos. Of course, the irony of this is that Jesus' melody was in complete harmony with the consistent message of the scriptures, which defined the faith of Peter and his people – but the harmonic forms had to be worked at to be heard and appreciated. It is a bit like hearing Benjamin Britten or Alban Berg for the first few times and trying to work out how this can possibly be spoken of in the same language as Mozart or Bach. Or, to change the image, trying to cope with modern jazz if you have grown up with Julie Andrews and Cliff Richard. There is a consistency, but it is not immediately obvious and has to be worked at – which is precisely why Jesus taught in parables and invited those with the ears to hear to tease out what he was driving at.

What, then, was Peter to make of Jesus in the Garden of Gethsemane refusing to use violence to resist arrest and lead the revolution that would usher in the age of vindication and liberation? He has shared the three-year journey with Jesus and the other companions, has listened to the stories and teaching, wrestled with the strange conflicts between his unquestioned world view and that being represented and enacted by Jesus. Furthermore, he has pledged undying and immoveable loyalty to his friend and mentor, promising that he would defend Jesus to the death. He has had to listen to words of rebuke from Jesus, even being compared to the Satan, and has had to learn the lesson of humility taught by Jesus in the upper room after the final meal they shared in the celebration and re-symbolising of the Passover feast. Still, however, the picture does not make complete sense to Peter, and Jesus does not seem surprised (or disillusioned) about this failure of theological integrity.

The problem for Peter, although he perhaps doesn't know it, is twofold. First, how is he to cope with the need to lose or surrender his illusions about his own self in order to be able to see and live more transparently? Second, how is he to allow the 'Story' to be re-shaped when such a re-telling may assume denial of the original 'Story' and, therefore, denial of the God whose story it essentially is? When Peter's story is told, it is usually narrated in such a way as to focus on his denial of Jesus; but that denial was only part of the problem of denial for Peter. The threat and challenge for Peter to be converted in his mindset and world view (literally, to repent, from the Greek *metanoia*, a change of mind) is neither simple nor trivial; for the grasping of (or being grasped by) the ways of Jesus will mean letting go of (or denying) the hitherto assumed truth about God, the world and himself. It is too superficial merely to say that Peter let Jesus down at the crucial moment, but that his post-resurrection restoration and pentecostal empowerment made it all right again. The New Testament texts do not allow such a reading.

The gospel-writers tell us that Peter, despite his brave words of loyalty (a promise of blood loyalty was not a matter of mere sentiment or bland words in the culture of Peter), lost his nerve when questioned about his own identity by a young girl following the arrest and torture of Jesus. For a grown man to hide before a female was shameful; it represents an abject failure of intent and exposes the truth about Peter's character: now where is the rock-like quality that Jesus had (apparently mistakenly) identified some months earlier? Is this the sort of personality on which Jesus would be careless or misguided enough to build his *ekklesia*? But, when Peter's failure to stand with Jesus is exposed, his illusions of self-sufficiency die away with the embers of the fire around which he was warming himself when the girl approached him. And this disillusionment was bitter, its message one of hopelessness.

When Jesus met Peter on the beach (once again not in the place of religious worship, but back at his place of work) after the resurrection, he encountered one who had collapsed and whose understanding of God, the world and himself was shredded. The agonising generosity of Jesus must have been painful to bear as events now resonated unmistakably with earlier experiences of vocation: Jesus invites Peter to walk with him again up the same beach on which they had first met. And here again Jesus invites Peter to be his friend, journeying with him into another unknown world in which the previous certainties have evaporated. The only difference between the first encounter on the beach and this second one is that Peter has lost his illusions; he remains Peter, and he doesn't re-write his story in order to sanitise it.

The embarrassing fact is that Jesus does not ensure that Peter has grasped the full significance of the messianic revolution and the newly ushered-in kingdom of God. All he requires at this point is that Peter has lost something. Fear of denying the truth about God, the world and himself as he had received it perhaps led to him denying knowledge of and allegiance to Jesus; but this denial is now part of who Peter is. It is not just an embarrassing part, but an essential element of his make-up. Never again will Peter be able to stand in judgement on those who fail Jesus. Experience has taught him that, when it comes to grace, forgiveness and restoration, he is the prime recipient.

One could say that, contrary to our assumptions about what Jesus intended in describing Peter as a rock, he was saying something possibly offensive to religious people's self-righteous sense of strength and power. The strength of character which Jesus is seeking in his friends – however long it takes them to discover it – is not proud or arrogant, but rather is rooted in grace, born out of the ashes of failure and issuing in humane humility. This rock is not solid and impervious to sensibility; it is not hard-faced, forcing weaker objects to bounce off it or shatter against it; it is the sort of rock on which a building can be erected because it can be relied on to cope with the underlying movements of the earth and the battering of the elements around it. There are many forms of rock, and this one appears to be more limestone than granite.

Peter, then, had to endure the pain of denial and loss. This involved denying friendship with Jesus; but this, paradoxically, was the door to finding genuine friendship – friendship without illusion – with Jesus. The loss and denial are integral to the process, and there appears to be no other way. Those who want to see in Peter the story of a man for whom it all worked out neatly in the end will have to do violence to the story as it is told in the gospels, the Acts of the Apostles and the letters, if they are to hold to that illusory view. Jesus saw Peter's denial as the way to allegiance, not as the end of a friendship; for any relationship must be dynamic, any journey unpredictable, any transformation costly.

Facing the truth about our stories

This ineluctably brings us to the point where we must consider the import of denial for ourselves, the church and the world in which God has put us. As individuals, we should derive from Peter's story great hope and gratitude. For Jesus chooses the weak and the fickle, allowing them to be themselves and to take their time. He takes raw human beings with all their illusions and distorted theologies and invites them to walk with him on a journey the end of which is unclear. He is not surprised by failure and weakness, but sees the inevitability of the same for those who in the end will have the strength of character that only comes through positive disillusionment and humility in the face of failure to be what we know we ought to be. But this journey with Jesus may be costly and painful, driving us to face the challenge of denying/losing God in order only then to find him – or, indeed, find that he has already found us. We can relax when faced by Jesus because he does not have the illusions about ourselves that we have, and he sees the potential for what might be rather than being limited by the reality of what is. Like Michelangelo and his massive rock, he sees not the hard and impenetrable exterior, but perceives the angel waiting to be discovered and released – even if it takes hammers and chisels and sweat and pain (and the incomprehension of outside observers) to do so.

For the church of God, this notion of denial must be grasped if she is to reflect the character of the Father, Son and Holy Spirit she claims to represent. In owning the mixed history of the church and identifying with it, we cease to pretend that the church's cruelty, bigotry and misguided wickedness at many times and in many places of this world's story are someone else's problem. The massive benefits brought by the Christian Church to the world (the drive which led to modern science, for example) should be celebrated and taught, but they must not blind us to the reality of Christian betrayal, denial and failure to fulfil our calling to be God's people for the sake of the world. It is stupidly naïve to think that the Christian Church can ever be dissociated from particular cultures and histories and no longer have to struggle with the problems of inconsistency and the potential for arrogant bigotry (even when dressed in the language of humility and grace).

However, in having the courage to learn and own its story, the church must also learn from the Jesus whom it follows that his kingdom is playing a different tune from that of the world in which we live. A church that pursues or clings to power as Herod, Judas, Peter, James and John, Caiaphas or Pilate understood it must face the pain of disillusionment and loss. For Jesus, power is found in letting the powers do their worst and refusing to collude in the fantasy that might is right, that success is the ultimate vindication, or that beauty assigns greater value than ugliness. The cross becomes the place where the messianic pretensions of the powerful bleed to death, only later to find a re-interpretation that finds meaning in service. But it is only by recognising the failure of the church to fulfil her vocation that denial can be integrated into conscious experience and an honest telling of the story and ultimately make of the church the sort of rock that Peter was.

Like the early Philippian church, contemporary Christians may need to surrender any claim to spiritual rankings based on social status. Theological orthodoxy is to be sought not as an acquisition that confers accept-ability and defines who is 'in' and who is 'out' of the pilgrim people, but rather as a prize that will only be recognisable once we are known as we are and we see face to face. The church needs to allow people the space to start on the journey with Jesus and his friends, perhaps not even spotting the potential, but always running the risk that both Judas and Peter find a place among us where they can see what Jesus is up to in the world and attempt to comprehend it. Indeed, the church must create the space for people to encounter Jesus and take their time in walking with him. It must find imaginative ways of letting people hear the invitation of Jesus to walk with us and him, neither prescribing each step of the journey nor setting tests of allegiance at every turn, but denying the power of certainty and embracing the humility of grace.

This will always be costly, because the church – any church – will need to recover the calling of service and the humility that comes from experience of loss. It will be painful, because it means relinquishing control of people in the church, their theologies and thinking, and encouraging them into a dynamic pilgrimage in which a messy people walk with Jesus and try to see the world through his eyes and feel it through his touch. If the priorities of Jesus are to be owned by and reflected in the life of his church, then his people will have to face the reality and truth of their own messy story, have the courage to confront the fantasies of religious or spiritual power and reject the sort of power-play that characterised James and John and their ambitious mother.

Only thus can the world be served and saved. The church will have its Peters and its Judases, probably in equal measure. The wheat will grow with the tares, and that is how the church in the world is and always will be. There will be ambiguities and uncertainties, and some people will deny the wrong things. Yet the church might become the community in which people can own and not deny their stories, facing the truth about themselves and others, no longer afraid of that truth and how it might be handled by other people. Ultimately, maybe, the church will be able to cease playing God and allow people to join the journey, letting Jesus be Jesus, letting his words resound and his healings surprise and scandalise those who think he has departed from the script that we would prefer him to follow – usually one which places us with the sheep and not with the goats. Of course, the moral of that particular parable is that the goats always thought they were sheep, and the sheep had no idea they were anything. He that has ears, let him hear?

Chapter 5

SILENCE

Jesus and his companions are in the process of having their world demolished in the most agonising way. It is not just that this Jesus who had promised so much had seemed to court disaster, but also that they now find themselves exposed to the same potential fate. It is possible, however, that even now, with Jesus under arrest and abandoned by most of his male friends, he might pull some unforeseen rabbit out of the hat and confound his enemies after all. Being put on trial would at least give him an opportunity to make his case definitively and be judged accordingly. Wouldn't it?

The trial of Jesus must have been deeply disappointing. For, like a lamb before its shearers is dumb, so did Jesus choose to remain silent before his reluctant Roman judge, Pontius Pilate. The judges who came from his own tradition and culture had found him too threatening and had decided on the verdict before they confronted him with the charges. It should be remembered that, never the consummate diplomat, Jesus was known to have referred to such power-brokers as 'tarted-up tombs', cultivating a public image of ritual and, therefore, moral cleanliness and respectability, but being rotten and putrid inside. These were people who had been publicly and shamelessly accused by Jesus of being overbearing and demanding rulers, heaping unbearable burdens on ordinary people as a means of spiritual, cultural, economic and political control. There was no love lost here, and Jesus found himself consigned to the courthouse of the Empire.

Reading the gospels

Before looking more closely at the confrontation of Pilate with Jesus, it is worth pausing to consider how we read these gospel narratives in the first place. The immediate problem faced by anyone who is remotely familiar with the stories is that of an assumed single reading of the text. That is to say, we filter the story through the framework given to us by the readings we have heard, possibly since childhood and on through sermons and so on. This means that the reader or hearer unconsciously ceases to be open to a different reading, one which might open one's eyes to new details or perspectives that might make us think or see differently. A simple example of this is the parable already referred to in this book and known as 'the prodigal son'. Helmut Thielicke made the point that this title by itself makes us focus on the wrong point and the wrong character in the story. This is, he argues, the story of 'the waiting father'. Whereas the story has been used for generations as a depiction of the errant son's repentance and reception by his father, even a cursory reading of the text reveals that the son's motive for returning has little to do with acceptance of guilt for appalling behaviour and much to do with selfish scheming to save his own skin and play on the good nature of his father. As the son makes his way back from the foreign place where he has squandered his wealth and ended up with the pigs, he works out his story and polishes the words (and no doubt the whole act) which he will use when confronted by his father. This isn't repentance as it is often understood by evangelists and preachers; it is scheming self-preservation.

However, as we have already noted, the father's behaviour would have been shocking to the first hearers of the story and ought also to be to us: the father abandons all convention and respectability, all sense of justice and discipline – he has been waiting for his son, looking for him (every day?), scanning the horizon in the thus far forlorn hope that he might one day appear. On seeing his son in the far distance, he gathers up his skirts, baring his legs, and runs out to meet his wayward offspring. What is so shocking about this? Respectable men did not expose their legs, did not run anywhere for any reason and would preserve their dignity by punishing the son appropriately (which in this case would mean at the very least a refusal to have his son back as a son, let alone to welcome his return); there was a price to pay for the offence that this son had caused not only to his father but also to social convention and, therefore, to the wider community.

However, it could be argued that even Thielicke missed the point. Should this parable actually be termed 'the parable of the self-righteous brother'? In the form of this story, Jesus is clearly aiming at the religious professionals who have a well-developed and highly detailed system for relating to God and society, but are missing the point of it all. Instead of this system being a means to an end, it is as if fulfilment of every jot and tittle of the law has become the end. Jesus illustrates in a shocking and exaggerated way how the father's love is scandalously, even offensively, generous, and contrasts this with the response of the one who, having lived with and tried to please his father for years, shows how calculating *he* has been and how little he has learned of the real nature of the father. In common with other parables and real encounters with the religious authorities, Jesus indicts those who claim allegiance to God and his character while not reflecting that character in themselves, their own lifestyle and priorities. Neither son knows nor understands the character or motivation of their father.

This is a recurring theme throughout the scriptures, especially in the prophets of the Old Testament. Consider Jonah, for example, and the lengths to which God goes in order to convince the reluctant prophet that his nature is to be gracious and generous, calling the people of Nineveh to repentance. Jonah refuses to preach repentance to Nineveh not because he is afraid of them, but because he doesn't want them to repent and change their ways. He wants them to get blasted to smithereens by God. This would have the wonderful effect of satisfying Jonah's bloodlust (and that of those whom he represents), justifying his racism and vindicating his theology. The story is well known: God pursues him, even through the vomit of a large fish, and eventually Jonah gives in. He reluctantly and churlishly goes to Nineveh, says the words and turns to leave. To his horror, the people respond to the call to turn back to God, and their repentance is real and deep. Did Jonah rejoice at this fruit of evangelism? Did he marvel with newly opened eyes at the extravagant and long-suffering grace of God? Did he celebrate the unexpected response of aliens to his God? No! He was embittered that the Ninevites hadn't got what they deserved – fire and brimstone. Even at the end of the story (which should always be read in one sitting), Jonah cannot bear the fact that God is graciously generous to Nineveh. Jonah wanted and, despite the things God has shown him, still wants God to be just ... and obliterate Nineveh from the

face of the earth. The story ends with Jonah not learning about grace.

The generosity of God is offensive to those who are
self-righteous, and his mercy transcends even justice. It
will be clear from this, then, that how we read even a
very familiar parable will determine how we see God
and the point of the story. Much traditional preaching
of 'the prodigal son' ceases to ring true once one has
heard a different and more complete reading of the
story. This is true of many passages and stories in the
Bible, but perhaps nowhere more true than of the
Passion narratives, where familiarity can blind us to the
surprises which lie at the heart of them.

It would appear that Jesus has been brought to trial
before the Roman authorities in order that they should
take responsibility away from those religious people who
wish to achieve an end without having to be burdened
with the guilt of it. What follows is intriguing, although
the synoptic gospels differ in detail from the longer
account given in the fourth gospel. In particular, among
all the many threads one could follow in these rich and
powerful narratives, three features of the accounts stand
out as remarkable: first, the three times (according to
Matthew) that Jesus responds to questions of identity;
second, the silence with which he judges his captors; and
third, the echoes between the cries of the crowd and the
temptations which Jesus faced at the beginning of his
ministry in the desert. We shall take each in turn.

A question of identity

According to Matthew, Jesus responds to three questions
using the same words. Judas (26:25) is among the twelve
disciples at the last supper together when Jesus tells
them that one of them will soon betray him to his death.

65

Naturally they protest; this must have been a devastating and bizarre statement by Jesus at a moment of dramatic poignancy. Judas responds, 'Surely not I, Rabbi'. Jesus replies, 'You have said so'. Later (26:63), in the house of Caiaphas, the high priest charges him, 'I put you under oath before the living God, tell us if you are the Messiah, the Son of God'. Jesus replies, 'You have said so'. Then (27:11) Pilate the Roman governor asked him, 'Are you the King of the Jews?', and Jesus replied, 'You say so.'

It is one of the features of Jesus' ministry that he makes people take responsibility for the judgements they make – especially judgements about who he is. Jesus once asked his friends who the people were saying he was, and received a variety of answers ranging from John the Baptist to Elijah the prophet. But he then compels them to make their own judgement, committing themselves to the identification to which they attest. For Peter then to say, 'You are the Messiah of God' was no trivial play with words. Peter had made the claim and must now be judged according to it. The rich young man came to Jesus and asked what he needed to do to inherit eternal life, only to be told what he did not want to hear: Jesus told him to relinquish his security and invulnerability and join in the journey with him and his friends. The young man considered the option, but decided this was not for him – at least, not for now – and went away. Jesus did not run after him offering easier terms and conditions, but rather let him go to be responsible for his own judgements and decisions. Throughout the gospels, Jesus refuses to take responsibility for other people's commitments, knowing that adults have to own their own decisions and choices and not be allowed to escape into a fantasy land in which responsibility is relinquished and God (or someone else such as the vicar, the Church, liberals, evangelicals and so on) can always be blamed when things turn bad.

And so it is with Judas, Caiaphas and Pilate. They make their statements and Jesus bounces the question back, demanding that they make their judgement and stand by it. Thus, Judas condemns himself with his own words; it would have been better for him if he had remained silent. Caiaphas must judge whether or not Jesus is the Messiah of God and then live with the consequences. And Pilate must draw his own conclusions about whether or not Jesus is the King of the Jews and what that might mean for Jesus, the people, himself and the Empire he represents. It is not surprising, then, that when we read the gospels properly (not in little disconnected bits, but as whole narratives written to tell a story and pose a question), we find ourselves being asked not only to join Pilate in saying, 'Here is your king' (John has 'Here is the man!' in 19:5), but also to address for ourselves precisely what that statement means. Jesus will not do this for us; we must make our own judgement about who he is and then live accordingly. Of course, it is possible to use words loosely, even with the best of intentions, and not mean what is said – witness Peter promising undying loyalty to Jesus shortly before denying he ever knew him.

The power of silence

Why does Jesus then stay silent before his accusers? If the charges are trumped up and he is being misrepresented, then why does he not fight for truth and justice? Does he not owe it to his friends and the people for whom he came and whom he has defended from the dehumanising power of religious authority to speak up and argue his case? Or is his silence merely attributable to the absence of an argument, a lack of confidence in his calling or his own identity? There is another way of looking at this, of course, and that is that Jesus, paradoxically, neither acknowledges the power of the court nor believes himself to be the person on trial.

Sometimes words get in the way. In any trial in any court, individual words will be picked over, analysed and used in evidence against the accused. Language will be deployed skilfully on each side to nail or defend the person in the dock. So, words become not only means of explanation or alibi but also hostages to the fortune shaped by those whose job it is to find evidence and prove a point. Silence in court may be taken as an unwillingness to incriminate oneself either validly or inadvertently and may be interpreted as an admission of guilt. But silence is capable of other interpretations.

Jesus stands before the representatives of religious, moral and ethical power and refuses to play their game according to their rules. This is utterly consistent with everything we have read in the gospels, from healing (the wrong) people on the Sabbath (the wrong day) to re-interpreting the law given to Moses. He then stands before the political and judicial representative of one of the most powerful military empires in the history of the world and refuses to collude in claims about who has the greatest power and authority. The silence of Jesus represents a refusal to play the world's games on the world's terms.

The reason for this appears to be that Jesus considers not himself but the world to be on trial. In this perverse context, it is Jesus who is free and the representatives of what the apostle Paul later calls 'the principalities and powers' that are bound. Both the religious and political empires deal in violence and death, getting rid of those who are awkward, doing whatever is necessary to maintain the status quo and protect the locus of power. As is always the case, the 'powers that be' do sometimes believe that this way of running affairs is the best way for everyone because it guarantees social and moral order and establishes a sort of stability. (There are, of course, echoes of this in the unintentionally ironic use of the language of 'freedom and democracy' during the bombing in Iraq of the people for whom 'liberation' was to be imposed and 'democracy' delivered through catastrophic violence ... whatever the people actually wanted. As some journalists pointed out at the time, this irony would be compounded if the Iraqis went on freely to choose a dictatorship by Islamic fundamentalist theocrats, thus testing just how far the west really believes in 'democracy'.) But history demonstrates that injustice breeds resentments which poison generation after generation and feed the violence of the wronged. Any account of history shows that violence breeds further violence and that there comes a time when God's people must refuse to play the world's game on the world's terms. The kingdom of Jesus does not work this way, and there will be a price to pay for living the life and values of his kingdom in the present world order, where silence may be taken for weakness.

This is why it is the world and its ways that cannot see that it is they who are on trial before Jesus and not the other way round. Faced with his silence and refusal to collude, the empires and powers have no recourse other than to deal out more violence and yet more death. Before the one who judges all our values and ways of living, who questions by his silence the terms on which we see the world and its history, the empires are impotent. Pilate may fear a popular uprising and the consequent problems with Rome and may feel that appeasing the religious rulers is a small price to pay for peace. But he turns over an innocent man to his death, washes his hands and tries to absolve himself of responsibility. Yet, as we have seen, such responsibility cannot be ducked, and Pilate stands alongside those who bay for Jesus' blood, on trial before the silent judge, the one who knows where true power lies and where the world's powers will surely lead.

What sort of kingdom?

The gospel accounts of the trial of Jesus cannot fail to resonate with other elements of the gospel stories. There is a consistency about Jesus' ministry in word and deed and in the way he faces this dreadful dénouement. We recall that, after commencing his public ministry at his baptism in the Jordan, Jesus was led by the Spirit out into the desert to be tested. He had to face then – and had to face subsequently many times, including at his trial – the fundamental question of what sort of kingdom will be his. Will he compromise with the compulsion to satisfy material desire at all costs? Will he test God by creating miracles and invoking legions of angels in order to play power games and ensure that he is protected from the realities of life and human existence? And, finally, will he compromise with the 'powers that be' in what we have called 'playing the world's games according to the world's rules' – in this case, arrogating power to himself for the best possible motives and in the process colluding in the fear-born fantasies of the powerful people of this world?

Here, before his accusers, Jesus faces these temptations again. Having set his mind on the values of God at the beginning in the desert, he now endures the inevitable consequences of consistency. It seems to those witnessing these horrendous events that the kingdom of this world has in fact proved itself to be more powerful than that of Jesus. It appears that the kingdom of Jesus spells out weakness and failure and a loss of nerve, silence leading to execution. The bloody finale will now be played out before people who are either relieved that the flame of grace has been snuffed out before it could light a possibly inextinguishable fire, or in despair that the glory they have longed for and thought they had witnessed in Jesus had come to nothing – yet another disappointment, another tragic loser with messianic fantasies who ultimately offers a lot but delivers nothing other than pain.

The truth, however, is that what appears to be the negation or denial of hope is in fact the means of hope. The world stands on trial, unwittingly and arrogantly; but the truth will not be suppressed, even by death on a cross. God's kingdom will be vindicated and his power will prevail, not in ways that the world will judge to be attractive or valuable, but by the transformation of the world through this man's death and later resurrection. What has been described as the world's 'myth of redemptive violence' is deposed by the 'myth of redemptive suffering'. There are still Pilates and Caiaphases who cannot or will not see this and persist in incredulously asking of Jesus and his people, 'Do you refuse to speak to me? Do you not know that I have power to release you, and power to crucify you?' (John 19:10). But Jesus, hitherto silent, knows where power really lies and will not collude in the fantasy of the judges who do not realise that it is they who are being judged.

A time for words, a time for silence
All of this comes as a warning not only to the power-brokers of the world and those who assume (or are

given) religious authority over people's lives, but also to anyone who claims to be a follower of Jesus. For it is too easy for us to blame those whom, out of our own sense of personal powerlessness, we set up as targets. We can all find ourselves responsible for colluding with 'the empire'. It was not just powerful people who struggled to distinguish between the two competing melodies sung by Jesus and the 'powers' and seemed unable to pick out or recognise the former. It is perhaps not surprising that what Jesus did by his actions and words, both healing and challenging, he continued by his silence and still offers to anyone who will look and listen: that is, he offers to 're-grind the lens behind our eyes', helping us slowly and gradually to change the way we see God, the world and ourselves, seeing through his eyes more clearly and more nearly as we are converted in body (our lifestyles and behaviour), mind (our world view and the values we live out) and spirit (our identity as God's grace-born children, the identity that makes us both who we are and whom we shall become on our journey in companionship with Jesus and his friends).

Two illustrations come to mind: music and drawing. A musician friend of mine described his band's new acoustic album as being 'full of holes ..., silences that cry out for notes, but demand that we live with the emptiness'. Nature may abhor a vacuum; but music sometimes compels us to live not just with the notes we hear but also with the gaps and intervals that give shape to the whole. One of the things that budding artists have to learn early is that you can either draw an object or draw the spaces around the object, thus allowing the form of the object to emerge. This demands a new way of looking and seeing and describing. It is not something that appears obvious to a non-artist; but, once grasped, it opens up new ways of looking at the world.

These two examples illustrate something of the importance of silence and space. That is, they emphasise the necessity of looking not only at what fills our lives but also at the spaces and gaps and emptinesses. The truth of the matter is that these spaces (or silences) allow shape to emerge and music to be heard that could easily have become crowded out by noise or things.

Jesus uses few words before his accusers and judges. He allows for space and silence and encourages both them and us to live with the silence, see what shapes emerge from the observation, and hear the echoes of another world resonating in the refusal to fill every silence with comfortable and comforting noise.

There are times for words and times when silence speaks louder. There are times when the questions of the curious and the bewildered need simply to be expressed, but not immediately answered. There are people who must be left to discover the answers for themselves because to answer their questions for them will be unhelpful, allowing them to avoid the responsibility that comes from discovery and recognition. The desire to control the answers which people are given (sometimes despite the actual questions which they are asking) is powerful and too easily grasped by religious leaders. Jesus gave people the time and the space and let them live with their conclusions. It is likely that he has not changed his mind on the matter and still invites us to invite others to join in the journey and see what happens along the way. It will be surprising and sometimes shocking, but it will be silent in the face of threat and life-giving in the face of death.

Chapter 6

MOCKERY

Probably the most ignored commandment of the ten given by God to Moses and notionally adhered to by Christians everywhere is the ninth: 'You will not bear false witness against your neighbour'. This might also be rendered: 'You will not misrepresent your neighbour's case'. It is not so hard to spot the theft of your neighbour's ox or ass, and murder is hard to cover up; even envy and covetousness are not easily hidden. It is a very different matter, however, when it comes to dealing with the ninth commandment. For the evidence of the Christian Church is that we happily criticise each other, set up Aunt Sallies in order to knock them down, misrepresent each other's case, gossip about human failure (usually sexual), identify the worst in our neighbour in order to pull him apart and bolster the sense of our own rightness. We also do it to other faiths: although most Christians would object strongly to having Christianity represented by Northern Irish sectarianism, they still demonstrate little reservation in characterising Islam (and, therefore, all Moslems) as suicidal fundamentalist terrorists who all look like Osama bin Laden.

In one sense, this reaction is very human and all too understandable. Fear often makes us vulnerable, and we then cope with our own insecurity by identifying some-one or something that we are not in order to damn the other and reassure ourselves. This is true in the sphere of international politics, sport and just about any other human activity. But understanding it as such does not let those who claim adherence to the Ten Commandments off the hook of culpability. It is a mystery to many outside the church how Christians can be so obsessed, for example, with sex that any sexual sin is targeted pitilessly while envy, greed or misrepresentation are pretty well ignored. From time to time, clergy will be asked to withdraw the sacraments from someone whose sexual behaviour is the source of suspicion or gossip; it is doubtful if clergy have ever been asked to withdraw them from gossips, malicious misrepresenters or those who exaggerate to the point of lying. Why the inconsistency? To use a relatively recent illustration, how did some evangelicals in the Church of England manage to damn the newly appointed Archbishop of Canterbury for his views on human sexuality and yet do so in a way that was disingenuous, ungenerous and often misrepresentative of his case? Or are some of the Ten Commandments of higher status than others? Is God more passionate about stamping out some of the sins than others – indeed, are some of the prohibited behaviours to be ranked as 'first-order' and others as 'secondary' offences? And before this paragraph gets misquoted, let us be clear that inconsistency of practice does not negate the importance of any one commandment; failure to be consistent with all ten does not mean that no comment should be made about the breach of some or any of the others. But whoever speaks of the sin of another must do so with grace, generosity, discretion and love – and with the humility that comes from observing through the eye with a plank in it the splinter in the eye of the offender.

The plea here is that Christians should demonstrate in their public utterances the generosity and accuracy called for by Christ. Otherwise they should keep as silent as Christ was when he deemed it appropriate. For, when Christians behave badly towards each other, they bring into disrepute (and render incomprehensible) the gospel of reconciliation to which they claim to have responded in faith. In the contemporary world, as in the world of Jesus and Paul, the gospel itself is enough of a stumbling block to people; it is tragic that the good news of the Christian faith itself is frequently obscured by the bad news of Christian loose tongues. The task and vocation of the Christian community has always been and always will be to live out and proclaim the good news that God in Christ is reconciling the world to himself – not to fight or undermine each other through distracting disputes over every iota of ecclesiological detail or theological dogma that emphasises 'our soundness' over against its lack in others. One has to question the (unconscious) motives behind what might be called 'bacon-slicing' approaches to theology or statements of faith that are used to define more and more finely who is 'in' and who is decidedly 'out'.

Scandal

For the church, there is already enough to contend with. Christianity itself is a scandal. The word comes from the Greek *skandalon* and means a stumbling block. This is what Paul refers to in 1 Corinthians 1:23 when speaking of Christ crucified being 'a stumbling block (literally, a "scandal") to the Jews and foolishness to Gentiles'. The Christian gospel appears both absurd (when judged by the values of this world) and dangerous (when seen through the eyes of powerful people, especially powerful religious people). Jesus was not nailed to a cross by the Roman Empire in collusion with the Jewish establishment because he recommended a theology of niceness and polite relationships; rather, he was crucified because the melody he was playing was threatening the integrity of another harder, louder melody and exposing its seductive siren appeal. Jesus questioned the way the world is and dared to suggest that it might be different – indeed, must be different. But the challenge to the status quo, coupled with the alternative which he recommended, were perceived by many as, literally, scandalous.

There are occasions in the gospel narratives when the reader feels a certain sympathy for the Pharisees, chief priests, elders and scribes. They constantly try to set Jesus up, even to the extent of using distressed people's lives as a tool for winning a theological argument. Their constant frustration with Jesus will resonate with the experience of anyone who has tried to have a theological discussion with someone who constantly refuses to accept the premises of the debate. There is a sense that, each time they come to him (or send people in their place), they can't suppress their excitement at having set the ultimate trap for Jesus. Yet, either through statement, question or silence (cf. John 8), he manages to turn the argument round or embarrass the plotters in public.

It was with some relief, then, that they eventually found grounds on which to take him into custody and get him put on trial for his life. The trapped had now become the hunter, the prisoner the jailer. The mood turned harder and more grim – the darkness deepened, as John puts it in his account of the events leading up to the crucifixion. Jesus, they think, is now no longer in a position to wriggle and humiliate his enemies as he has appeared to do in the past. The game is up, and the fearful authorities can now smell blood. Of course, the real tragedy of this whole business is that it is precisely those people who are most concerned to serve God who find Jesus most difficult to understand and who ultimately insist on his demise.

The problem of incomprehension

Christianity is a stumbling block, a scandal, for many reasons. For those who accept a world view in which might is right and power is something to use for gain, the notion of power being found in weakness is absurd. For those who see Pilate as being the powerful representative of imperial greatness, having the power of life and death for those who are brought before him, the sight of a bedraggled northern builder-turned-preacher being nailed to a cross will not be appealing. For those who think that death, violence and destruction always have the last word, the silence of the accused will always appear to be wilfully and stupidly suicidal. And to those who believe that beauty, image, success or material possessions give them their value in the world, the idea that exposure of the real person beneath it all can be ultimately liberating will be perceived as dangerously threatening.

What frequently happens when human beings are threatened with exposure, weakness, silence or suffering is that they ridicule the one who brings the threat. It is always easy to spot when an argument is being lost because the loser will sometimes turn to ridicule either of the argument or of the person who is deploying the stronger argument.

Human beings can turn very quickly from total commitment to an idea or person to ridicule and rejection of them. The friends of Jesus, as we have noted, swore undying and unconquerable allegiance to Jesus, only to abandon him and deny knowledge of him within a matter of hours. And the crowd that had heralded the coming of Jesus into the city only a few days earlier, waving palm branches and shouting 'hosanna!', now turned against him, appealing for his execution. It is not clear what brought about the change; but it could have been disappointment, the unbridled need to see some action, the misrepresentation of Jesus (as a dangerous fraud) by the religious authorities or simple rent-a-mob tactics. Whatever the cause, the fact is that the mood of the people turned in a very short time from hopeful acclamation to a cynical cry for blood.

It is easy to read through the details in the gospel narratives and uncritically pass over the ridicule of the soldiers and those glad to see Jesus get nailed. The religious leaders incite the crowd to hatred and violence (Matthew 26:67; Mark 14:63–5), and the crowd happily responds as desired. The priests and soldiers use Jesus as a plaything, the dehumanised object of their power games (Matthew 27:27–31; Mark 15:16–20; Luke 23:11–12; John 19:2–3). The words and claims of Jesus get twisted and turned against him, deliberately misused and deployed as tools of ridicule (Matthew 27:39–44; Mark 15:29–32; Luke 22:63–5; Luke 23:35–8). Yet these examples of ridicule should make us pause for reflection. Surely there are many in this world who have been the victims of religious leaders using their influence to incite their followers to violence and hatred – and no religion holds a monopoly on this sort of abuse of people (compare, for example, Palestinian Moslems and Israeli Jews). The Crusades saw slaughter and bloodshed as a price worth paying for power and possession of land. Christians have used the cross as a symbol of war and power in ways which are indefensible in terms of the gospel. It is not unknown for Christians to use the Bible in general and the words of Jesus in particular as weapons with which selectively to attack one another and seal their differences in blood and venom. And, each time this happens, we once again spit at the vulnerable Jesus, mock him and ridicule him, beat him and condemn him and his people to the ways of cynicism, violence and death.

It is significant that Jesus is silent in the face of this abuse. He does not engage in theological dispute over what he really meant when he spoke of the Temple being destroyed, nor does he insist that his accusers define their terms more closely. There comes a time when ridicule and mockery have to be absorbed silently because they are born not of rational conviction but of fear and bewilderment. And, although it is tempting to answer every charge and correct every misrepresentation, it is sometimes necessary simply to take the beating and feel the spit on the raw skin, knowing that the time for verbal defence has passed. This will sometimes make the Christian community seem stupid. We will appear to be useless at defending the truth and standing up for what is right and godly. But a judgement has to be made with the wisdom of Christ as to whether this is the time for words or the time for silence.

One example might suffice to illustrate the point in the context of a contemporary society in which the media (principally the printed media) are powerful to the point of being an almost unaccountable new priesthood. When the film of Nikos Kazantzakis' novel *The Last Temptation of Christ* was shown in the UK, the Christian community to a large extent made very noisy and ill-informed objections. Despite the fact that the film was based on a fictional idea and that the whole point of the novel was to explore the humanity of Jesus being torn apart on the cross, the evangelistic potential of the product was missed. It was, they said, blasphemous and dangerous. Moreover, they claimed, it cannot be shown because it simply was not true. But the film takes more seriously than many Christians the logic of the incarnation: if Jesus was fully human, then he was also a fully sexual being; if the New Testament is right, he was tempted in all respects as the rest of us are; what, then, might this mean for this Jesus now dying on the cross, but able (as the temptations in the desert and the discussions in the Garden of Gethsemane make clear) to escape the torture if he so wished? The point of the novel and film is that Jesus faced this enormous temptation to choose the easier way, leave the cross and live his life with Mary Magdalene as his wife, but chose not to do so. So, how powerful is that?

The somewhat hysterical protest, accompanied as always by placard-bearing cinema pickets (who, of course, hadn't seen the film), achieved the remarkable result of making the film and its contents more widely known than it or they might otherwise have been and encouraged some people to view the film who might otherwise not have bothered. Judgements on the quality of the film have been very mixed, but the whole business illustrated how, perversely, the apparent vigorous defence of godliness just made the Christian community look silly: fearful of any argument, unable to understand the role and purpose of the arts (it *was* a novel, after all), unwilling or unable to think about sexuality in a rational way, and so unconvinced of the ability of the faith to stand up to scrutiny, searching examination or ridicule that it must be protected at all costs. (Witness also the reaction at the time to Monty Python's *Life of Brian*, Denys Arcand's *Jesus of Montreal* and more recently to Mel Gibson's *The Passion of the Christ*.)

Jesus demonstrated that you have to pick your battles and recognise the *kairos*, the appointed time. Is it not significant that, according to the gospel-writers, Jesus defended and restored dignity to the women with problematic sexual histories, but turned over the tables of the men who made these women what they were? Jesus defended the women who had been ridiculed and abused, but was unwilling to mitigate his contempt for those who bought justice, played hypocritical games with other people's lives and otherwise misused power, especially religious power. As Tom Wright, Bishop of Durham, has said, 'Two thirds of the world cries out for justice while the other third talks about sex'. Maybe we ought to get our priorities right – which means getting them in line with those of Jesus.

Scandal within the church

The gospel of Jesus will always be counter-cultural and scandalous to a world that has bought into a different script. But to get our priorities right and in line with those of Jesus will inevitably mean causing scandal within the church itself. It is a sad fact that, if the same people whom Jesus healed and embraced came the way of the contemporary church, they would not necessarily find a welcome in our midst. They might soon be made to feel unwanted because of the judgements of those who lead or preach within the community of faith. Those whose lives are messy or inconsistent will need to find understanding, love and grace. Furthermore, they will need to find Christian churches that create for them the space within which change of life might be nurtured over time (in other words, repentance) and dignity be always guaranteed. For, as we have seen, Jesus simply called people to go with him on a journey and allowed them the time to misunderstand him, struggle with his behaviour, question his motives, disappoint him, deny him, betray him, abandon him and even call for his blood.

It is probable that if the church (and there *are* churches which are glowing examples of the priorities of Christ) creates the sort of communities in which such people feel comfortable, they will be less programmatic, messier, less tidy places. All sorts of heresies will be voiced because people know that ideas and passions have to be voiced in order to be confronted and tested. A community that says, 'Believe this and you can come in' is a community that wouldn't recognise Peter, Judas, James, John ... or, dare I say it, Jesus himself.

In some parts of the world, Christians experience dreadful suffering and persecution on account of their faith. Although they find themselves silent and voiceless, they do not understand the silence of those who might speak on their behalf. It is possible that we Christians in the comfortable western world are so preoccupied with our own navels (fighting the battles of luxury) that we fail to see the pain of our brothers and sisters elsewhere. It is a mystery why some western churches assume a siege mentality when there is no need and no siege. 'Suffering' and 'mockery' are relative terms – and getting a bit of stick in the media for Christians looking stupid in television soap operas is not the stuff of martyrdom.

It is possible that the Christian Church in the affluent and comfortable western world is too concerned about being the subject of ridicule and mockery. Some Christians only feel happy when they are being persecuted or made to feel miserable. And there are those 'guardians of the faith' who are so concerned to protect God and his gospel that they demonstrate a lack of faith in the power of this same God. Not for them the silent enduring of those who face the ridicule that 'your faith doesn't work', summed up in the cry of the crowd who will take Jesus seriously only if he 'saves himself'. The experience of the psalmists bears sometimes tortured witness to the silent response of God to the taunting ridicule of God's beleaguered people by their pagan opponents. From the gospels, a parable immediately comes to mind in this respect.

Matthew warns his readers about the need to be prepared for the coming of God as king. So, in his gospel, Jesus tells several stories, one of which concerns a man who decides to go away for a while and leave his servants with his property. He gives them varying amounts of money and responsibility and goes on his way. When he returns after a very long time (during which period it is possible that the servants thought he was not going to come back), he calls each of the three servants to account for their stewardship of his property and money. Two have used the money he had given them and have made it work for their master. The third has simply buried his money in a hole in the ground where it would be protected from harm, wastage, misuse or theft. The first two servants receive praise; the third gets thrown out. Why?

Well, to address the question of protection of orthodoxy as seen through the lens of this parable, God is a risk-taker. The gospel does not have to be protected by being dug into a hole where it can remain pure and untouchable. God commends his gifts being subjected to all the risks and hazards of the big wide world and all it contains. Simply to build defences around the received dogma and keep it pure and unchallenged attracts the scorn of the master. Yet it is not that the third servant's tactics have *lost* the master any value; it is, rather, that they have been born of fear and conservatism. God's way, as demonstrated unequivocally in the scriptures, is to risk everything, letting the gospel and the calling of his people be subject to the chances of the real world. He comes among us as a vulnerable scrap of humanity, grows up in occupied lands with high mortality rates, and has a short-lived (unsuccessful and unremarkable) public ministry in a very limited environment. He is subject to the perverse whims and fickle affections of human beings at a particular time and place in the world's history. In short, he risks everything and lets it happen.

Is it not remotely possible that God wants his people to stop cushioning his good news? Is it not 'biblical' to stop dividing God's people around questions of narrow (and highly selective) definitions of 'orthodoxy'? Does God want his people to be so faithless that they cannot allow the gospel to be subject to public scrutiny and – yes – mockery? Are God's people to be so afraid that their gospel won't survive that they have to defend God at all costs? Or does this same God call his people, made in his image, to risk everything by exposing the gospel and the scriptures to a mocking world and engage with that world, learning to see why it mocks in the first place, not simply misrepresenting its case, but responding to it in faith and love?

At his trial and on his cross, Jesus was exposed to all that the world could throw at him. And he didn't throw it back. He absorbed the pain and demonstrated again that God takes a long-term view of these things – even mockery and humiliation and death and resurrection. Mockery might not have the final word in this world, but there is no need to be afraid of it or to strive at all costs to avoid it. If the good news of God in Jesus Christ is true or credible or worth believing and living, then it must be able to stand the scrutiny of the academic, the adversary, even the mocker and flogger. Like Jesus, the mockery might be met with silence or a refusal to collude in the fantasy or to argue on the basis of the presenting assumptions about God, the world and people. But the gospel does not need to be protected, buried in a hole, preserved in its pristine condition, preserved from any contact with a dynamic life which might challenge, hone or re-focus it. For the power of it will not be contained by theologies or ideologies, cannot be suppressed – even by suffering and death. And the laughter of the mocker, met by the silence of truthful grace, will run its hollow course and dry up in embarrassment.

To live is dangerous – as God in Jesus found out. For the gospel to live is also dangerous. But God is a God who risks everything and commends those who do the same. His people will always appear to be reckless, misguided or absurd, and these may possibly lead us to a cross and the silent appropriation of other people's violent spit. We should not go out looking for trouble or misinterpreting incomprehension for persecution, especially in order to reinforce our own religious identity or prejudices. But this is the way of Jesus and might be the way of those who accompany him. After all, he did say that those who wanted to go his way must deny themselves, take up their own cross and then follow him.

Chapter 7

DEATH

It is all too easy to speak of death in the abstract without having experienced the impact of it. We now live in a generation in which it is perfectly possible to grow into middle age or beyond and never to have experienced the loss of someone close. Contrary to earlier ages and cultures, it is probably true that most people in the developed western world have not seen, touched or smelled a dead body. Perversely, the same people are subject to hundreds of 'deaths' every day on television, film and computer games, deaths from which you simply move on, often unmoved and unaffected by the deathless and consequence-less death you have either witnessed or perpetrated. There is no pain, no loss and a numbed perception of what death involves and represents. Yet all this contrasts with the truly terrible experiences of millions of people in the world every day who suffer famine, disease, torture, oppression and avoidable death and loss.

This must raise questions about contemporary western understanding of what was involved in crucifixion. It is a common experience in churches on Good Friday to find the crucifixion narratives leaving people feeling that they ought to respond in a particular way, but feeling as if the whole story is somehow distant and removed from them. And this poses a considerable challenge to clergy and those who order liturgical worship on such occasions – especially when there are children present – to find ways of explaining what crucifixion meant and represented, how crucifixion might be understood today and how the events of the first Good Friday might be perceived and received in a different and distant age, place and culture both spiritually and emotionally. This considerable task is not helped by the sanitisation of death in the west and the evolution of the symbol of the cross into an icon of popular jewellery now divorced from its original signification (as the girl in the jeweller's shop asked, 'Do you want a plain one, or one with a wee man on it?').

In a culture that venerates beauty, youth and success while trying hard to avoid impairment, age, failure and death, it is difficult to persuade people that life is to be found right here where the suffering is acute and death a terrible and cruel reality. Jesus' notion that we only find life in dying to our self appears to be as experientially absurd as his belief that 'the first shall be last and the last shall be first'. Life as we know it (or wish to believe it to be) is just not like that. In one sense, there is nothing at all new in this; the psalmists frequently bemoan the fact that the wicked seem to prosper and those who strive to be faithful to God's calling continue to suffer.

The other problem is that the cross has become a theological construct through which so much Christian theology is seen, but the integrity of its place in the gospels themselves can get lost. Ask any group of Christians why Jesus was crucified and died, and a range of answers will be forthcoming, each of which indicates the particular theological and spiritual lens through which that person sees the event and its ongoing significance: he died to forgive us our sins; he died because the Romans wanted a scapegoat in order to keep the peace; he died because the Jews wanted to keep power; he died so we might go to heaven; he died as an example of selfless sacrifice to show us how to give of ourselves; he died to make us good; he died because he had an almost suicidal death-wish and stupidly refused to defend himself just when it mattered. The list could go on, thus demonstrating that the answer to the question is determined by what answer you think the question is asking for. (This is not to imply, however, that there is simply a single answer to the question.)

The cross of Jesus needs to be re-signified by a church that seems sometimes to have lost its ability to explain its theology in terms that are comprehensible to ordinary secular people. The only way to engage in this semiotic task is, in fact, to return to the gospels and allow the cross to speak to us afresh in all its aspects and with all its voices, challenging us to open our eyes to see beyond the sometimes narrow perspective with which we have either come to or grown up in the faith. For Christian theology is essentially cross-shaped, and Jesus is clear (as are the apostles and the New Testament writers) that Christian living is to be understood in terms of incarnation, cross and resurrection. To sanitise the cross or allow it to be sanitised is to empty Christianity of its essential power and meaning; it is to tame Jesus and reduce him to an object of religious sentimentality.

Jesus and his fear

There are those who read the gospels as if Jesus went cheerfully through his last days, his macho brow furrowed with determination as he purposefully goaded the authorities into fulfilling his desire to be martyred. This is nonsense. Jesus struggled in the desert at the beginning of his ministry with temptations which accompanied him throughout his life and public ministry. In the upper room, while sharing what he knew to be his last supper with his friends, there is a tension in the air as he tries to explain what his friends were conceptually and emotionally unable to hear or understand. The pathos is almost unbearable as he leads his friends out to the Garden of Gethsemane to pray and, ultimately, to lose his freedom. Here in this garden – which is reminiscent of a garden in Eden – Jesus, the new Adam, faces again the powerful human temptation to duck the challenge and the pain and find an easier way. Faced with suffering of an excruciating kind, he prays to the Father whom he loves and with whom he knows himself to be at one and cries for a resolution to the conflict between his human fear and his Father's will. Once again, he is confronted by the familiar dilemma: the way of suffering or the way that allows you to satisfy your material human needs and desires as your first priority? The choice, as in the desert earlier, is very real, not simply a matter of rational discrimination or a notional calculation of the pros and cons of each option.

Clearly, even for Jesus, the one who could call down legions of angels to protect him, death was something to be feared, a dark night into which one should not go lightly. If Jesus was truly human, then the taunts of those who wished to neutralise him by ridicule and humiliation will not have been empty or without power. What if he had got the whole thing wrong? What if he were to die and find it had all been a needless mistake? Is there *really* no other way of handling all this? The fear is palpable, the dread all too real.

What happened on the cross?

Jesus is finally nailed to the wood of the cross and the structure is dropped into its hole, wracking his body – already weakened by torture and abuse – and tearing his joints. And from this vantage point, high and lifted up, exalted (but not in the way people expected the Messiah to be high, lifted up and exalted) and surveying the people who have put him there, he says some remarkable things.

According to Matthew and Mark, he cried out in despair using the harrowing words of the psalmist: 'My God, my God, why have you forsaken me?' Jesus is not here simply indulging in demonstrating his memory for Bible verses while he has got a captive audience. Rather, he takes the words of the very psalm (22) that his people cite in worship as an expression of their corporate desolation and desperation for vindication and makes them his own, thus identifying himself with that people as their representative. Then he screams, expires his final breath and dies.

According to Luke (although not all ancient authoritative manuscripts have this), he says, 'Father, forgive them; for they do not know what they are doing'. These are words he could have used of the disciples throughout their journey together, but here they are directed at ordinary people who would be as surprised as the 'sheep' and the 'goats' in the parable (Matthew 25) to discover that all was not quite what it seemed. They long for deliverance, the end of their exile, the forgiveness of their sins (which is what the ending of exile meant – cf. Isaiah 53) – and the one who can accomplish this in them and for them is the very one whom they are crucifying as an imposter. They are killing the one who alone can give them life. And Jesus, knowing their confusion and limited comprehension and the fact that they, too, are frightened human beings, open to manipulation and power games, asks God to forgive them.

Luke then has Jesus promise the man being crucified alongside him that he will indeed accompany him in Paradise that same day. This man, dying an equally cruel and pointless death, has defended Jesus against the mockery of his fellow felon, understanding the irony of the situation. It is not clear, however, what the criminal understood by Jesus' promise. Crying with a loud voice, Jesus then says, 'Father, into your hands I commend my spirit', and dies.

John offers a different narrative again. Jesus looks down from the gallows and sees his mother and the 'disciple he loved' standing beside her. He commends them to each other as mother and son and creates a new family unit that breaches normal conventions and expectations of family responsibility and obligation. Indeed, a new age is being inaugurated here in which the old societal conventions are being re-interpreted and a new way of belonging is being opened up.

Jesus admits to thirst, and a branch holding a sponge soaked with wine is held to his mouth and he dies, claiming, 'It is finished'. Remember, however, that Jesus had previously told his disciples after receiving the wine at the last supper that he would not taste it again until he comes into his kingdom. So what might John be saying by this? Well, possibly he might be suggesting that Jesus is *now* enthroned in his kingdom – right here on the cross planted in the rubbish dump outside the city walls, where all the refuse was consigned to oblivion – but that his kingship doesn't look like most people would have expected. This, of course, brings us back to the account of James and John, close friends of Jesus, who asked to be placed at the right and left hand of Jesus when he comes into his kingdom. They clearly understood this to mean that they might be admitted to the places of honour and privilege, seeing kingship through the old lens of status and power. Jesus had responded that they would indeed one day take these places, but not in the way they had imagined. On the cross, he had someone on his right hand and someone on his left hand. But they weren't the people who would normally be depicted as sitting alongside the king. This, however, is not that sort of kingship capable of being described as 'normal'.

There is deep irony in all this. The place of agony, defeat, humiliation and death has become (though nobody there realises it) the locus of healing, victory, dignity and hope. The throne of this king is flanked by people not of honour but of degradation. In death as in his life, Jesus is surrounded by those who do not belong, those who are shunned and despised, those who are held to be of no value and no account in this world.

What James and John had to discover was that to sit at the right and left hand of Jesus was to share in his fate. It was to lose any sense of status or privilege and abandon any thread of attachment to the ways of this world or its values. To sit alongside Jesus the king meant losing your life and confronting your death. Stripped of all dignity and hope, here – at the end of all things – you would find the place of grace, the source of genuine glory, the glory as of the only-begotten of the Father. Here Jesus is exposed to all that the world can throw at him, and he does not throw it back; he absorbs it, takes the pain and the anger and the grief and the vitriol of the victim, and he dies in a whisper of selfless generosity towards an unlikely recipient of grace.

95

Apparently the ways of the world have been vindicated once again. As our contemporary media represent in full colour, we live in a world that repeatedly and consistently reinforces the message – the obvious and incontrovertible truth – that violence, death and destruction will always have the final word. There, on that miserable gallows, yet another victim of Roman imperial justice suffers the fate of all those who dare to question the dominant world view that asserts the ultimate power of power. In this broken body and silenced spirit, the old truth is proclaimed afresh: the ultimate enemy is death, and those who control its timing and condition are, indeed, the powerful of this world. So it has always been, and thus it always shall be.

Yet, as shall be seen later, this place of apparent confirmation proves to be the place of revolution – is this man's death really the end? Or is it the end of the old world and its cynical, defeatist miserable fatalism? The place of death opens the way to life. The place of humiliation trembles with the possibility that the end is but a beginning, that all is not quite as it seems. The place of total shame marks the end of a world in which violence and destruction evoke fear and claim the allegiance of those held captive by the power of their dogma.

It is hard to overstate the potency and horror of this scene for those who had accompanied Jesus through the last two or three years. Their hopes and dreams of a new world order lay bleeding on a Roman gallows. Their vision of a different way of glimpsing God and his life in the world hung helplessly from nailed hands and feet. No wonder the world went dark, the daylight disappearing in embarrassment at this apparent refutation of all that Jesus had promised about God and the future kingdom. Any illusions about vindication and the end of exile now lay broken and battered. The slavery will continue, and the disappointment will maintain its power. Death is final, and the latest hope of liberation lies exposed as a fraud in the dust of all the other let-downs and mad or bad losers.

It is perhaps unsurprising that the cross has become sanitised in western culture. Only a culture that faces the reality of death and smells its corrupting odours can understand the death of this Jesus. Only a people that faces humiliation and suffering can really enter into this story and know its power. And only a people that trivialises death on television screens and cannot cope with intimations of human mortality can turn this cross into an ornament. Only a church that reflects such a culture can possibly sing endlessly banal songs about this cross and this man's blood and turn the whole thing into religious sentimentality. The plethora of worship songs (usually to interminable and unsingably trite muzak) that speak of Jesus' death as healing and forgiving of 'my' pain possibly indicate just how empty the cross has become for many Christian worshippers: instead of being the place where 'I' am confronted by the truth about God and his weakness in the eyes of this world, Calvary becomes the place in which the western Christian tradition – compromised by the power of its uncontestable economic gods – claims its vindication.

This might seem harsh. But most of us live in a world in which we avoid death, mortality, contingency and temporality as much as we can. Despite what we sing in our hymns and say in our prayers, we associate God with the meeting of our desires and the comfort of our lives. Yet the cross rudely and embarrassingly over-shadows such superficial escapisms and challenges the squeamishness of a culture gone soft, a culture that can

97

only cope with horror and death by either romanticising them or pretending they only happen 'somewhere else a long way from here'.

The followers of Jesus had no time for escapism. Faced by the demise of Jesus, they found their brave new world brutally punctured. Any hope they had of seeing the Messiah crowned and his people liberated in their own land had evaporated. The hopes they had seen awoken in people who had been defended or forgiven or healed by this Jesus now lay shattered and breathless, now exposed as fraudulent. If creating an illusion in needy people is bad enough, to allow the illusion itself then to be destroyed is appalling. The hopes and fears of all the years are met in him this night – and shown to be mere illusions, wasteful fantasies, useless opiates used only to con the masses to believe that the world could be better ... when everybody knows it can't be.

If you want to see whether churches and Christian communities have understood the power of the cross of Calvary, visit them for the Holy Week and Easter celebrations. There are churches which live the story of Jesus and his friends and remember the hopes and agonies of this most awful of stories. There are also those which get to Good Friday, celebrate Jesus' victory on the cross, then move on as quickly as possible to Easter Day and the great resurrection celebrations. But they get there by theologising the cross and avoiding the crucifying agony and desolation of it. The story is told as if it were simply doctrine and merely concerned 'my' or 'our' personal forgiveness. Thus the power of the devastating disillusionment of Jesus' friends is avoided or overlooked. But the rest of the story does not make sense without our entering into the experience of those who had ventured to trust Jesus, who had accompanied him on his journey and witnessed his teaching and healings, who had dared to see faintly through his eyes ... only to find themselves desperately let down and betrayed.

In other words, the power of the apparent defeat of Jesus has to be faced and lived with. The apparent victory of the 'empire' with its creed of power, violence and death has to be admitted and respected. We have to have the courage to stand by that cross, look at that tortured man, face the obvious futility of life and hope, and contemplate going back into a world whose creed has seemingly been vindicated once again. Unless and until we have stayed there a while and faced the awfulness and desperation of that place, we cannot begin to understand what will follow.

In this way, the cross can only begin to become the place of healing and forgiveness for me and the world once I have seriously faced the power of the alternative world views, identified the scandalous nature of a God who lets himself be beaten, and recognised in the open arms of the dead man that there is no place for vengeance – that hope for the world and for me lies in the abandonment of illusion and the demise of any way of life that justifies itself by its avoidance of suffering and death. Here is the place where any wet-nosed theology of God making his people healthy and wealthy ultimately bites the dust. It is the place where we must choose which world we will live for and what sort of world we will create and shape.

Perhaps one of the most striking conflicts of recent times has been the incomprehension expressed by many in the west (including Christians and those shaped by Christendom) in the face of suicide bombers in the Middle East. How, scream the newspapers, can a young woman with intelligence, beauty and her life before her possibly blow herself up in an attempt to destroy the lives of other people she doesn't even know? How can someone see death (and the deaths of others) as something to be welcomed and embraced? What religious devilry is it that turns an otherwise normal young person willingly into a human bomb? Yet these questions betray a fundamental misunderstanding between people of totally different world views: for one, death is to be feared and avoided at all costs – the final and ultimate enemy; for the other, death is the gateway to another world in which the justices that are trampled upon by the powerful of this world are put right. No wonder that the west has had to re-think its military strategies in certain parts of the globe: it is not very useful to threaten people with the ultimate sanction of death if that death is perceived by the one threatened as something to be welcomed. The threat is not exactly likely to make the bomber hesitate before setting off the explosives.

However, the global conflicts which we see these days – conflicts not just of political, economic, cultural or religious world view – compel us to shine some light on our assumed understandings of death and its meanings. The individualism of the west and much western Christian theology and spirituality appears in stark contrast to the communal nature of eastern societies and faiths, and we fail to remember that Christianity is an eastern faith born out of Semitic cultures and headed by a young Jew. The reality of the belief that many Christians purport to have in life after death is tested by a western obsession with keeping people alive at all costs and seeing death as a failure.

This is reflected in the songs we sing. Wesley said that we learn our theology from the songs we sing rather than from the sermons we hear, and he is right. So if we sing rubbish, we will believe rubbish. Endless songs proclaiming triumphantly of Jesus that 'back to life he came' betray a belief in resuscitation, not resurrection. This Jesus died, was dead and buried. His body was embalmed and he was buried in a tomb. He was dead and could do nothing to come back to life. He was powerless. Dead. Breath did not miraculously come back into his lungs and his blood did not just start flowing again, reconstituting the cells of his body and reviving him. As we shall see in Chapter 9, resurrection was something God did. To wish that Jesus had come back to life is just one outworking of a confused fear of death and a collusion in the world's view that death is the ultimate enemy to be feared above all else. Christians should be a people who face death in all its vivid colour and fearful agony, not minimising its power, but seeing it through the eyes of Jesus who truly died and was buried. Christians should be a people who reject the pervasive, seductive and dominant culture which sees 'success' as everything and death as the end.

The cross is where Jesus the Messiah died. Really died. And it is the place where I and we can take a fresh and brave look at our own hopes and fears, our values and ways of living and seeing. It might be that this place becomes the place where I have to die also – and with me all the conceptions and comfortable theologies and pet values that Jesus hung there to expose in the first place. Until this place has truly been visited, we cannot go any further, and the story of Jesus and his friends remains just an interesting tale of gullible people being temporarily distracted by a charismatic entertainer and illusionist.

Chapter 8

EMPTINESS

Someone once described going on a journey with Jesus as being like a non-swimmer crossing a river on stepping stones – the only problem being that only one stone appears at any one time, and even that one slowly dissolves as the water runs over and around it. It seems that only when the stone has almost totally disintegrated and disappeared, threatening to plunge you ruthlessly and meaninglessly into the depths, does the next one begin to emerge, thus allowing you to go one step further. It seems as if there are no guarantees and no fixed route; there can be no going back, and yet the way ahead seems terribly uncertain. Like most of life, it is only when you complete the journey that you can look back and see which way you have actually come – and recognise both that it is probably not the way you yourself would have chosen and that you probably wouldn't have begun the journey if you had known not so much *where* it would lead you, but *how* it would lead you there.

This offers a contemporary insight into what it must have felt like for the friends of Jesus as the events of what we now call Holy Week began to unfold. It is clear from the gospel accounts that they thought the Passover celebrations were going to be different this year, but they equally evidently had not the faintest idea that the week would end in torture, death and the collapse of their new world order. One can only imagine the horror they must have felt as Jesus was first arrested, then tried, tortured, humiliated and executed. And not only did they have to cope with all that, but they also had to face the fact that, despite their earlier promises to stand by Jesus come what may, most of them had in fact deserted him and abandoned him to his merciless fate.

So, the interesting question here is: what happened on Saturday? The temptation for contemporary Christians is to run too quickly from Good Friday to Easter Day, missing out the Saturday experience. This, especially when enshrined in churches' liturgical or worship practice at Easter, is dangerous. For Easter Day means nothing and has no joy if Friday and Saturday are not experienced first, the horrors and questions being endured and lived with.

Staying with Saturday

There has been a horrible confluence of events. The Passover meal awakens and celebrates the hope and conviction that God will once again liberate his people, thus vindicating them, their story and their faith before the eyes of the 'powers and principalities' of this world. The companions of Jesus have begun to glimpse the strange possibility that their friend might just be caught up significantly in this messianic hope and that the time might now be right for the irruption of God into their time and space once again. They have caught sight and sound of a different way of seeing and being and, although not fully conversant with its language as yet, recognise that they have heard echoes of another country, one in which the promises of the prophets hint at fulfilment. But, just at the point where one might expect some of the pennies to start dropping, the whole business is torn apart, destroyed before their eyes. The hope-giver is rendered hope-less, and the echoes fade into the night sky, leaving them without consolation in a now frighteningly empty and silent world.

It is impossible to overstate just how literally world-shattering these events have been for the friends of Jesus. If the lens through which they see the world had been shaped in a particular way before the crucifixion, it was now being hammered into another form. The Messiah is not supposed to die. God is supposed to vindicate his chosen one and, through him, his people. The signs of messianic identity (healing the sick, giving sight to the blind, and so on) should now be authenticated by the Messiah's triumph over Israel's adversaries, thus leading the people out of their captivity into the freedom of a new 'promised land'. So, a dead Jesus surrounded by the bragging soldiers of a triumphant pagan state doesn't look quite right, does it? It wasn't supposed to end like this! Consider, then, the immense cost of allowing your entire world view to be radically re-shaped. How does a dead Messiah become a victorious king? How does the 'defeat of God' become seen as the vindication of God's nature? How does the scandalously shameful become the essentially hopeful?

The process of repentance (mind-changing) is not easy and certainly not romantic. It is brutal and costly, painful and tragic. It leads broken people deeper into agony and emptiness and, at this point, does not promise them any deliverance. And this, paradoxically, is the way of grace. There is no other path than this one. Grace may have brought me safe thus far, and grace may lead me home ... but grace might also lead me through this darkness and pain, and it will feel anything but merciful.

To understand this, we need to return to Peter. The charge of the people in the courtyard, that Peter was one of the friends of the man soon to be nailed to his cross, now takes on a more sinister significance. Would the authorities now begin a witch-hunt in order to identify and crucify those whose minds had been infected by the scandal-monger they had finally caught? Perhaps it is only now that the enormity of what they have been caught up in these last three years finally begins to dawn on them. All the things they have heard about the world hating them, about carrying a cross and denying themselves, about losing your life to gain it – all these and more besides now seem awfully real and very unattractive. How can this be happening? The script they had been following while events unfurled had assumed a different ending – and, if it had to involve death, it certainly wasn't supposed to be theirs.

So, what did the distraught, bewildered and frightened friends of Jesus do after Jesus had been executed and placed in a borrowed tomb? The answer is: we don't know. Luke tells us that 'on the Sabbath, they rested according to the commandment' (23:56). It is somewhat difficult to see what this 'resting' involved, given the events of the previous couple of days. Certainly, we can imagine them not doing a great deal; but it is impossible to believe that they simply reverted to their pre-Jesus life and did what they usually did (or didn't do) on the Sabbath. Did they go to the Temple and allow themselves to be exposed in the bright light of day as friends of the executed insurgent? Or did they simply hide in fear, confusion and disillusionment?

It is interesting and significant that the gospel-writers record only what was verifiable and did not see fit to insert details that weren't required. In one sense, the lack of any comment other than Luke's general one is symbolic of what we might imagine was going on in the minds and hearts of these people: there was an emptiness, a numbness shaped by bewilderment, fear and grief. A world has not just fallen apart; it has been brutally extinguished. And, to use the metaphors from earlier, it is unclear which melody is now to be heard; the stepping stone has disappeared and the next one has not yet emerged – and at this stage there is no indication (or hope?) that one will emerge.

Anyone who has mourned the loss of a loved one will know at first hand the 'Saturday experience'. The adrenalin-fired shock and disbelief of the immediate aftermath of the death makes the mind doubt the reality and finality of the loss. It might be difficult to sleep as the mind plays games, rehearsing the day, trying to re-write the history and make everything all right again. But, eventually, sleep comes, and the body and mind get some relief from the pain. The problem comes when you wake up for the first time in a new day and the naked, brutal truth of the bereavement cannot be hidden, the painful loss cannot be ducked: the person is really dead, the world has changed for ever and the future just looks empty. The immediate aftermath of a death can be easier to handle than the following day and days when reality sinks in. And it is the lack of an imaginable future that is most remarkable here – the fact that the entire shape of one's life, expectations, relationships and routines has changed in an instant and can never be recovered. The loss is agonising enough, but the lack of an imaginable future life is potentially terrifying.

This is what it was probably like for the friends of Jesus. We learn from the Easter narratives in the gospels that Jesus' bereaved friends stayed together, probably dreading the knock on the door that might herald the next round of trial, torture and death. The past three years had been hard enough to come to terms with, but the immediate future now looked bleakly empty, devoid of meaning and content.

The point of this is that the disciples had no option but to stay with the emptiness and live with it. They could not escape from it into the sort of activity which might allow them to run away and avoid the pain. The fact that it was the Sabbath meant that they would not have been able to travel – after all, Jesus was not with them now to embolden them to test the limits of the law in the face of suspicious and antagonistic Pharisaic lawyers. They are stuck with their grief, with nowhere to hide and nothing to do.

There is a fundamental problem with people who want to jump from Good Friday to Easter Day, missing out the emptiness of Saturday. We alluded earlier to bad liturgical practice at Easter; but the same can be said of whole communities as well as of individual Christian experience. The biblical narrative has this experience of 'waiting for the right time' at its heart; indeed, it runs as a leitmotif throughout the story of God and his people throughout the generations.

As we noted in an earlier chapter, when the people of Israel left captivity in Egypt after 400 years of growing oppression, they were still led by God to spend forty years in the desert, a time during which the 'captivity generations' died out and the people were prepared for a new life in a new place with new rules and a new way of being that particular people with their particular divine calling. The exiles could not rush their liberation, but had to learn to wait for God and his *kairos* (the 'right' time). When Jesus was led by the Spirit into the desert to be tested, he might have been tempted to get out of there as quickly as possible; but it was important for him to stay with the 'desert' experience and not avoid it. It is too easy to try to avoid the emptiness when it is only by living with the emptiness and fear that we can make any sense of what might follow.

A problem with our reading of the gospels (apart from the familiarity of the narratives) is that we read each episode in the knowledge of how the story resolves (resurrection, and so on). Thus we read too quickly and don't live the experience with the friends of Jesus, learning to understand that on that Saturday they had no idea what might happen on Sunday. They knew only that a life had ended, not that a new life was about to begin. And the experience could not be missed; it could not be avoided or escaped; it could not be rushed. Saturday has to be endured in all its horror because we will not be ready for Sunday until this has been done. Or, in the words that are often repeated but are nonetheless true, there can be no resurrection without crucifixion ... or the empty day in between.

Three observations may be made from this brief exploration of the Saturday experience: first, the importance of *kairos*; second, the communal nature of the experience; and third, the meaning of healing.

Waiting for the right time

There are churches and preachers today (as there have probably always been) who hold out the promise of instant spiritual gratification. God is just waiting to satisfy the needs and desires of our hearts and longs to make life nice for us – apparently. Events are advertised in total confidence that the worship will be 'powerfully Spirit-led'. It is questionable how far these promises and their underlying assumption of God's supine nature are evidence of a theology shaped by western consumerism. According to this way of thinking (and believing and praying), God is there to make our lives easier – regardless of the immense suffering of millions of earth's inhabitants who have little or nothing. But there is a hint of a suspicion behind all this that this notion of God and the world was precisely what Jesus felt he had to reject when he was being tested in the desert.

To put the question bluntly, where was this God during the 400 years that the Israelites spent in Egyptian slavery? What would your faith in and understanding of God be like if you had lived in a forty-year period beginning in, say, year 230 of that captivity – with no direct memory of past freedom and no remote hope of the liberation that will only come after another 170 years? How are we to understand the faith and experience of those who experienced the exiles of the sixth and eighth centuries before Christ? Was their God shaped by his willingness to satisfy their needs and make them happy? Or, indeed, did their faith in God depend on him even liberating them at their convenience?

Jesus repeatedly told people that 'his time had not yet come'. So, the urgency to make God act at the behest of human impatience is rejected. The biblical narrative is absolutely clear in describing a people whose hardest lesson was always to learn to wait for God. In the same way that the captive Israelites waited for the exodus and could not liberate themselves, so the disciples had to learn to wait for the *kairos*, God's time, and not try to force God's hand. This meant learning the hard lesson of taking a long-term view of life and of God. Their faith was to be rooted in the person of God, not in the delivery of a particular outcome. Yet it is perhaps not surprising that, in a world of instant access to information and goods, a world in which we need not wait for the seasons to produce their fruit because we can import whatever we fancy when we fancy it, the notion of waiting for God is not comfortable.

This notion of waiting for God also lies behind Paul's injunction to the Christians at Galatia to 'keep in step with the Spirit'. It assumes that the Spirit sets the pace and that the job of the Christian community is to discern and follow it. This takes the initiative away from us and gives it to God, thus requiring us to be attentive to God's activity in the world, discerning his word and work, and not trying to rush him. Wherever we look in the scriptures, we find the same message being reinforced by the experience of God's people. Again, post-exodus Israel spends forty years in the desert learning that God will not be rushed. The psalmists lament the loss of their land, but recognise that they have to stick with the experience of exile and bereavement. The prophets see clearly through the eyes of God and tell the truth about what they see and understand – but they still suffer the fate of their people. Their faithfulness does not exempt them from the collective suffering of their people – look at Jeremiah if this point is not clear enough. Jesus spends forty days and nights in the desert being tested about the nature of his kingship. The disciples spend three years learning (supposedly) what God, Jesus and the kingdom of God are all about ... and then it all apparently falls apart. Yet Jesus had already recognised that, with human beings, a long-term view is vital because they can't take in everything in one go. Jesus had to risk everything by letting the disciples experience the appalling loss of Good Friday and the shattering emptiness of Saturday before the surprising joy of Easter Day could be possible or make any sense at all. And the story continues like this right through the experience of the early Church.

So, if God can take a long-term view and work with the foibles, vicissitudes and limitations of ordinary people throughout history, why should we expect him to behave differently with us? The contemporary Church needs to learn to face Good Friday and then live with Saturday, resisting the urge to end the pain or short-cut the waiting for God. It is a lesson the Church shows little evidence of wanting to learn.

Sharing the darkness

The gospels indicate that the bereft disciples stuck together in their lostness and fear. There is no indication that they started to have a go at each other, voicing their recriminations about the weaknesses, inconsistencies or failures of nerve. The texts do not suggest that all the others had a go at Peter for being a pretty feeble rock, for deserting Jesus and being a hypocrite of the first order. James and John do not get the blame for having voiced their dodgy theology in aid of their own advancement of status. Thomas does not incur the wrath of the fundamentalists for wanting to be a little more cautious about how things were to be understood.

This Saturday of waiting was a shared experience for these people. They could not make sense of events as individuals doing isolated reflection. They needed one another – not because they could sew up all the loose ends and make a neat account of the world they were now living in, but because there was a place for simply being together with their shared and common experience of loss, fear and confusion. They were a theological mess, caught between theological world views that no longer made sense of the life experiences they were enduring. But they stayed together and, presumably, talked together, sharing their doubts and fears and humiliations.

The people of God need to do their theological reflection together, corporately, sharing their experience and doing their theology in the light of it. They cannot wait until it all makes sense and everyone can sign the statement of faith that allows them to belong. The theology has to be dynamic, being worked out as understanding and faith are shaped and challenged by our experience of the world. Only in this place of communal humility and commonly recognised emptiness can God's people be free to live with provisionality, endure the waiting time and be honest about the threat of the hard questions. Faith that avoids this experience is no faith. A Christianity that romanticises Good Friday before leaping to the 'resolution' of Easter Day is not the Christianity of the apostles. Rather, it is a fantasy, shaped in the image of a culture that too easily avoids reality and colludes with the myth of divine consumer satisfaction.

As hinted at in the previous chapter, one might usefully reflect on where the Church's liturgy and hymnody gives corporate expression to this experience of waiting and longing. If worship is to be real and to connect the worlds of God and human experience, then surely the 'Saturday experience' (with all its grief, questions, protestations and laments) must find expression in the worship of God's people. This is true not only because some people in our congregations will be at a place in their lives where there is no joy and where experience is characterised

113

by unresolved bitterness, sickness or confusion, but also because the whole congregation needs to have its theology shaped by the whole of human experience and challenged by those people and situations that put a question mark over the glib assumptions we easily make about God's blessing in our lives. A quick glance through the worship repertoire of many churches (including the most 'successful' and active) reveals that the 'Saturday experience' is not catered for and finds little or no expression. What, then, does this say about our theology and our view of the God whom we claim to worship and to whom we pray? Or do we no longer need to learn to wait for him, to live with emptiness and unresolved tension?

Healing the wounds

The Church is called to be a place of healing, a community where people can be honest and open, free to tell their story and not pretend. It is perhaps the only community in which human mortality can be faced openly and human inconsistency owned without fear of judgement. The Church, commissioned with a ministry of reconciliation, becomes a people who can be agents of healing because they are not afraid to name the pain. This community does not deny the agony of Good Friday or Holy Saturday, but can be unafraid to live with it, confident that the God who brought them thus far has not abandoned them – even if he feels very absent. As Jesus was led by the Spirit into the desert to be tested, so were the disciples led by God into the traumatic convulsions of these terrible two days.

For many people, the prerequisite of hope is the permission to acknowledge their sense of hopelessness without the threat of being judged faithless or being given a slick answer for the speedy resolution of this embarrassing lapse. The disciples share their fear and confusion. It will become clear that their Easter Day experience only becomes possible because they have lived together through Friday and Saturday. There are no short-cuts and no easy escapes. They have no option but to stop and wait and think and weep and wonder. In a culture obsessed by activity, drivenness, targets and success, perhaps the Church needs to recover the priority of waiting for God. It might look a little too relaxed, but it might be more godly and more consistent with its calling – to be the people of God for the sake of the world, called and caught up in the mission that is God's, a mission of healing and reconciliation for all God's people.

In recent years, the 'desert' motif has become a strong currency in Christian language and experience. Koyama's meditations on the 'three-mile-an-hour God' still speak powerfully into a Christian world in which results have to be seen and reputations made. He observes that the first thing that happens when you enter a desert is that you have to slow down. It is when you slow down to walking pace (3 mph) that you discover that this is the pace God has always been walking at. He ceases to be a blur as we rush through life and becomes a companion who walks with us in the arid places. The problem for most of us, however, is that we spend our time in the desert trying desperately to get out of it. According to Koyama, we must stay there, learn to slow down and meet God, live with the emptiness and solitude of the experience, and resist the temptation to be somewhere else quickly. For it is here that God is to be found, and it is here that we find ourselves to be vulnerable, naked and exposed – but not afraid.

This all says something about God and something about people. About God, it says that he is to be trusted even when the evidence tells another story. About people, it suggests that stubborn human beings need to learn to live with provisionality and emptiness, not being surprised by the apparent absence of God or the silence of heaven, but learning to wait and look and listen and discern – and to do all this together, humble in ignorance and inconsistency, but confident in the freedom to be honest and open. God's hand will not be forced and he cannot be bought – even by faith. It is just a thought, but what would it look like if we were now living in a period in which we were having to learn that age-old lesson of the desert: that we might have to spend years of emptiness in order to learn that we need God himself, not simply the answers to our prayers?

Chapter 9

RESURRECTION

The world has ended, and that is all that can be said. The disciples are holed up in hiding, locked into a rehearsal of the last couple of years' events. Lives transformed by Jesus of Nazareth have now met a bloody and brutal wall of death and silence. Their world has ended, and 'tomorrow' is not a word that means a lot. Jesus is dead and his body buried. All the words about God's kingdom and all the healings of sick and marginalised people simply stick out into the collective memory like a dirty needle scratching about in a painful wound. Have we been conned? Was it all lies and fantasy? Have we been embarrassingly and dangerously naïve?

Only once we have entered into the depth of the disciples' confusion and grief can we begin to move on to the experience of Easter Day.

There is much confusion among many Christians about the resurrection of Jesus from the dead. Some of the confusions stem from the temptation to read the gospel narratives with the benefit of knowing how the story ends up, instead of living the experience with the disciples whose stories are told there. Occasionally the Church has a screaming fit about a bishop's heresy regarding the resurrection, but these reactions often prove to be the result of theological and linguistic knee-jerks produced without the benefit of any attempt to understand the case being put. Thus, accusations fly around and God once again has to be defended from any deviation. Furthermore, some popular understandings of the resurrection often do not bear biblical (let alone rational or theological) scrutiny. As we observed earlier, one popular Easter song proclaims of Jesus that 'back to life he came'. The New Testament is clear that he did not.

Paul makes it clear that 'God raised Christ from the dead'. Jesus did not somehow get resuscitated in the tomb, his breath swelling his lungs and the decomposing molecules of his body reconstituting themselves beneath the shroud. Jesus did not simply come back to life and restore the *status quo ante* of his incarnate being. God raised Christ from the dead. It was God's initiative and God's activity. Jesus was completely dead and physically decomposing. This was no illusion and certainly not (as a former Bishop of Durham so eloquently and misreportedly put it) a conjuring trick with bones. It was God who acted and raised Jesus to new life.

Even a brief glance at the gospel narratives makes this clear. The Jesus who appeared to the stricken and surprised disciples was the same, but different. There was continuity and discontinuity. They recognised him, but weren't sure. This Jesus could disappear and walk through walls – unlike the Jesus of their three-year journey. Yet this raised Jesus bore the wound marks from his torture and crucifixion. What is clear is that, according to the biblical witnesses, the Jesus who emerged from the tomb was the same and not the same as the Jesus whose dead body was laid in it two days before. The risen Christ has a new body which is in continuity with his old body, but not simply a resuscitated group of cells and molecules.

The point is this: resurrection is what God does. It does not simply happen to Jesus, reversing all the horrible things that had been done to him and cocking a snook at those who thought they had defeated him. It is the initiative and activity of God who brings new life out of what is truly dead and helpless. That is why resurrection speaks primarily of who God is and only secondarily of who Jesus (in the judgement of the disciples) might be.

The recognition of this understanding of the resurrection of Jesus is important. For one thing, it will stop us singing silly songs about Jesus coming back to life and make us write songs about God bringing him to new life. It is no wonder that even Christians get confused about their own death, resurrection, heaven and all that might follow. The key to understanding Paul's conviction that God will raise his people from the dead (1 Corinthians 15, for example) stands firmly on the foundation that God raised Christ from the dead and will, therefore, do the same for those who are 'in Christ'.

This is also vital to a reasonable and consistent understanding of the gospel accounts of the encounters between the risen Jesus and his devastated friends. Despite his hints and teaching about his death and resurrection, their response indicates that they did not expect to see Jesus alive again. They had seen with their own eyes that his body was breathless and dead. They had laid his dead body in a borrowed tomb and seen it sealed. The tomb had been guarded by Roman sentries. And that was probably the end of the matter for the disciples. Wracked with grief and bewilderment at their dangerous and world-shattering predicament, they obviously could see no further than their current overpowering dismay. So, for Mary Magdalene to discover an empty tomb on the Sunday morning was to have misery compounded by further horror. Was crucifixion not enough for these Romans? Have they now had to take his body and desecrate it further, possibly for their own personal or political entertainment? Mary did not go to the graveyard looking for a walking, talking ex-corpse.

One of the things that characterises the gospel accounts of the resurrection appearances is their honesty. Propaganda would not and could not be written like this. Not only is nothing said about what happened in the tomb of Jesus (what might be called the 'observable mechanics' of resurrection), but the mixed reactions of the various disciples are recorded in all their confusion. Some believed it was truly him, but others were not so sure. Not only did they have to wrestle with the fact that he seemed to be back among them (the same, but different), but they also had to do some theological gymnastics. The world they knew and assumed to be constant had been interrupted. Their world view was being prodded around, and their assumptions about God and the world were being rudely challenged. And, even after the resurrection appearances, people like James and John were still not getting the point about Jesus' kingship and what it might mean to sit at his right and left hand. Even with the disciples, there is continuity and discontinuity: their characters and personalities do not seem to have been radically and instantly transformed by their experience of the risen Jesus, and the obsessive status-seekers remain preoccupied by the same questions that bugged them before. In the Acts of the Apostles, the post-pentecostal Peter is still recognisably the pre-crucifixion Peter of the gospels.

It was observed earlier in this book (in respect of the birth narratives) that our familiarity with the gospel stories easily blinds us to the bigger picture. Hence, we focus on the Magi's gifts of gold, frankincense and myrrh, but fail to ask why the gospel-writer has *these particular people* (pagans, outsiders, Gentiles) coming to pay homage to Jesus and recognising what the sleeping world of his own people fail to see. The same is true of the shepherds on the hillsides: why *them* (the uncouth who, because of their work, don't often get to church and therefore are not ritually clean)? Likewise, when we come to the resurrection narratives, we easily focus on one or two details and miss the question the writer might want us to address: why did he appear to *these* people in *this* way?

Is it not profoundly significant that it is to a woman that the risen Jesus first appears? Women, held to be of little account in that culture, figure so strongly in the biblical narrative that there must be a rationale behind their prominence. The genealogy of Jesus includes prostitutes and pagans. Mary is told she is to give birth, but she is just a peasant girl in a northern backwater. On the journey to Jerusalem, Jesus heals women who have been discarded from the community because of their health or reputation. Where others only scorn and sneer, Jesus touches and embraces and brings new life and dignity. He gives a name to a nameless woman (Luke 13) and humiliates the self-righteous (religious) men in front of the women whom they have enjoyed humiliating (Luke 7:36–50). At the cross of Calvary, it is the women who stay and watch and accompany Jesus to his death and grave. So, perhaps it ought not to come as a total surprise when it is to a woman such as Mary of Magdala (about whom a plethora of legends have grown up) that the risen Christ appears.

It is doubtful that Jesus was being ironic when he responded to a shocked Mary by telling her not to be afraid. But it is deeply touching that his first words were of concern for her. As with his encounter with Mary and Martha following the death of their brother, Lazarus (John 11), in which he starts with their need and takes the distinctive nature of their personalities seriously, so with Mary Magdalene he starts not with theology but with humanity. And so this woman is commissioned with the news of resurrection and sent to tell the good news to the world-weary men. She does not first have to submit to an examination in order that Jesus can check that she has correctly understood the meaning of resurrection. He sends her out with all her continuing confusions and tells her simply to say what she has experienced. That is all. She is not required to persuade or convince, just to tell her story and let the others make of it what they will.

In having Mary Magdalene be the first person to meet the risen Jesus, maybe the gospel-writer is ramming home the point illustrated throughout the gospels that it is often those who 'belong' who fail to see clearly who Jesus is for. It is those who love God and study the scriptures most fervently who are in greatest danger of missing the point that those scriptures are concerned to make: that grace belongs to God, that God is extravagantly gracious, that the kingdom belongs to surprising people, that these surprising people are usually also surprised people, that God will not be told to whom and in what ways he should be generous. So here, after the raising of Jesus from the dead, it is a woman, this woman, who meets him first and is called to do the priestly work of ministering that grace to those who are still hiding in their fear and shame.

The post-resurrection encounters are deeply moving in their simplicity and gentleness. And it is perhaps in the case of Peter that the poignancy of these encounters is most powerfully experienced. This is the man who had sworn that he would go to the death with Jesus. This is the man who had been re-named 'Rocky' even though the name didn't fit his track record. This is the man who abandoned Jesus at the end and disowned him before a young girl in order to save his own skin. This is the man to whom most of us would have given a post-resurrection hiding, rubbing into his raw shame the inconsistent and pathetic failure that he had become. Where's the bravado now, Peter? How big actually is the big man when questioned by a young girl? Isn't the name a bit of an embarrassment – shouldn't we re-name you 'Sandy' because you just crumble when the pressure is on?

Well, this is not how Jesus handles broken people. He doesn't rub their noses in the dirt of their failures. He doesn't need to build himself up by putting other people down. He doesn't wait until Peter is grovelling enough, repentant and weepy. Instead, Jesus meets Peter where he first met him three years before, at his place of work down on the beach. In other words, he goes onto Peter's territory and meets him there, where Peter is familiar and comfortable.

That is grace.

Peter is invited to walk once again up the beach with the Jesus who had first met him there three years before. But this journey is different. Jesus doesn't confront Peter with his failure; he invites him to express his love. Jesus does not deride him or remind him of his weakness. When Peter responds, Jesus takes him at his word and, without reference to what has gone before, commissions him to be the person Jesus knows him to be and take responsibility for the continuing community of Jesus' people. Three times Peter had denied knowing Jesus, and three times Jesus allows him to 'know' him with his own words and from his own lips. Thus is Peter restored and commissioned.

But there is more to say here. For Peter has not changed a great deal. This is the same man who had let Jesus down in the most devastating way, a man whose protestation of allegiance should not be taken seriously, a man who cannot and should not be trusted. However, Jesus does the unthinkable and trusts him. Why? Because Peter no longer has any illusions about himself or his own self-sufficiency. His self-respect and all the illusions about his strength have been shredded in the most humiliating way, and he is now stripped of any pretence. And this disillusionment becomes the key to his character and his trustworthiness. He is not suddenly strong and able to keep up his image; rather, he now no longer has to hide the fact that he is weak. In other words, he has been liberated in the most gentle and poignant way to be himself, accepted and trusted by Jesus. He no longer needs to pretend to be something he is not

And that is grace.

Thomas also finds himself taken seriously by the risen Jesus. Unsure of what he had been told (and, possibly, because of *who* had done the telling), Thomas needed a bit more evidence before he would believe that Jesus had been raised from the dead. When Jesus stood before him and invited Thomas to touch the wound marks of crucifixion in his body, the disciple had seen enough. But, again, Jesus does not humiliate him or argue him into a corner. As with Mary Magdalene, Peter, Mary and Martha and all the other gospel people, Jesus starts with the person Thomas is and meets him on his own ground. He does not criticise Thomas for questioning or for not being as ready to believe as some of the others.

Thomas is met in all seriousness and spoken with in a language he could understand.

And that, too, is grace.

All these encounters speak powerfully to those of us who have given up trying to keep our image intact and our theology perfectly formed. The sheer loveliness of Jesus' meetings with these devastated and humiliated people is utterly consistent with his handling of 'the poor in spirit' during his ministry and his proclamation of the kingdom promised by the prophets for so long. The arrogant and the proud found no place with this Jesus, and those who lived to preserve their power or status simply found themselves exposed and embarrassed. To be made transparent (the 'nakedness' of Adam and Eve in Genesis 3) is a threat to the image-conscious but exhilaratingly liberating to the humble. The journey to Jerusalem had ended in horror and the debilitating emptiness of death and bereavement, but now a new light was shining into a future that remained unclear and uncertain. The only certainty now was that God had proved he was on their side and wanted them as they were, meeting them on their own ground, taking them seriously as the people they had become.

It is not too great a leap to suggest that the people of God should still find themselves met by this risen Christ in this way. But it also follows that the community that bears his name should bear some resemblance to the Jesus raised by God who met his friends with such generosity and grace. The Thomases of this world might not need to be argued into a corner, but simply to be shown some incarnated generosity. The Magdalenes of this world might not need to be told how sinful they are, but simply find themselves told not to be afraid and to tell others of their own experience of a God who trusts even them. The Peters of this world might not need to be reminded of their failures and inconsistencies, but to be given the space to lose their fear and illusions and know they are trusted anyway.

Bishop David Jenkins once summed up his 'creed' thus: 'God is. God is as he is in Jesus. So, there is hope.' Surely that was the experience of these first witnesses of the raised Christ. They found in this Jesus the truth about God – and they also discovered something of the way in which God handles vulnerable people. No wonder they became a community of people no longer worried about their own life and death, but one of hope, whose revolutionary gospel compelled them to share the grace they had received by living graciously in the world of this God's making.

Resurrection was not just about what happened to Jesus. It was also about what this Jesus did with and for his friends – and how he did it. They discovered – as they had done on the journey to Jerusalem prior to Jesus' death – that if you take Jesus seriously, he will also take you seriously. They also discovered that the journey doesn't end where the world thinks it does, but that it continues into unexpected places. And, just as the initial journey with Jesus meant leaving behind some of the securities and familiarities and self-images and obsessions that characterise our little lives, so the encounter with the raised Christ means further loss and leavings.

Encountering and following the risen Jesus means letting go of our illusions about our own strengths and weaknesses and allowing ourselves to be transparent, no longer needing to hide. And the community of the church is called also to reflect the priorities and openness of

Jesus in its dealings on his behalf with the broken people of his world. The selfish and the arrogant will never find Jesus or his people comfortable companions. The proud and powerful will never trust the motives and integrity of people who see the world differently and honour the meek and humble. But those whose experience of life has deafened them to the good news of God's liberation will begin to hear the faint echoes of God's love. Those who have been blinded to the beauty of God's image in them will begin to detect the contours of a new embrace. Those who have been crippled by the constant battering that life brings them will find the hand of extravagant love being extended to touch, lift and support the weak limbs until the muscles begin to strengthen. Those who have been imprisoned either by the reputation others have given them or the self-hatred they have afforded themselves will find a door opening and an also-wounded hand beckoning them towards the light of freedom. And so it is that the call of Israel, summed up by Isaiah and read out by Jesus in his first sermon prior to being fulfilled in his person, is to be enfleshed by those who bear the name of the risen Christ in each generation. Christians are called to be Christ-like for the sake of the world.

This brings us back to the experience of Mary and the other disciples who are met by the risen Jesus with the words, 'Don't be afraid'. It sounds easy, it echoes comfort. 'Don't be afraid.' But it is murderously difficult to obey. Mary and her friends might justifiably have been afraid, for people do not meet risen dead people every day and have conversations with them. But those first words of Jesus – words of command as well as of comfort – have a wider resonance still. To be confronted by Jesus is to be invited to let go of the things that bind and trap us in life. If we are held captive by a world

127

view in which God is determined to hammer us into submission to his will, we might need to hear his words, 'Don't be afraid'. If our experience tells us that we can never escape our reputation or the secret shames of our lives, Jesus meets us and says, 'Don't be afraid'. When we are terrified about what people might say about us or do to us (especially if they knew the truth about us), the Jesus who has been there says, 'Don't be afraid'.

Letting go of our fear is, however, risky. It is easier said (and preached) than done. For there are some people and some things of which we should rightly be fearful. To expose one's inner being to other Christians can sometimes be an invitation for others to gossip. It might also lead to one's role in the church community being questioned or removed. There are people who will exploit what appears to be the weakness of others, sometimes without realising what they are doing. But it is also possible that our fear is directed at Jesus himself. What if he lets us down or abandons us? Where will it leave us if we let down our barriers born of fear and find ourselves naked and ashamed? What if we pin everything – life, hope, future – on Jesus ... and he goes and dies on us, leaving us alone and vulnerable in a hostile world?

Resurrection is the context in which these fears are to be owned and released. This Jesus has gone through hell, and God has not abandoned him to the grave. This Jesus can invite us to set aside our fear and trust him simply because he is here among us ... again. Don't be afraid of what the world can throw at you, says Jesus, because it threw everything at me and, look, I am here with you, newly alive, raised, wounded.

The challenge, however, is not just for the individual to reject fear and risk everything on the loving invitation of this Jesus; rather, it is for those who bear his name and call themselves his people to offer the same invitation to broken people in their midst and beyond. If the church is truly (and truly to be seen and experienced) as the body of this same Christ, it must surprise people in graveyards of fear with words of release and hope. Can the church truly advertise itself as a community or place where people can lose their fear and encounter the wounded and risen Jesus? Or will they find their fears increased (about God and his people), their shame exploited and their courage dissipated? Will they find themselves among friends who have walked this way, too, and understand the power of received grace and mercy, or will they find people playing religious power games which, despite the language of grace, speak of self-righteousness and justification? In other words, will the church be experienced as a community of graced people or an organisation of people who heap on weak and fearful people burdens they cannot bear? Jesus invited people to let go of their fear; his people should surely do the same, sound something like him and look like an approximate image of him as he is seen in the gospels of the New Testament.

Wounded hands touching wounded people, demanding nothing and inviting only a response, are the proven hallmarks of grace. And that was the experience of those who lost themselves on Friday, waited in desolation through Saturday, and found themselves to be loved on Sunday.

Chapter 10

FACING JERUSALEM
(AGAIN)

Experience tells us that many people find it easier to talk about themselves or things that matter if they are doing something else at the same time. For example, walking with a group of friends in the hills allows for conversation to be at times frivolous, at times deeply personal, at times intense. The context and activity also permit silence without embarrassment and the freedom to change the subject, move on to someone else or to simply look around and talk about the weather. This can be more fruitful than sitting in a room in a chair opposite someone whose attention is focused on you alone and who will not be deflected from the subject in hand. This is one reason why pilgrimages have been rediscovered in recent years by some unlikely people. As Chaucer celebrated so vividly and funnily in *The Canterbury Tales*, people talk while they walk and tell stories while their lives bounce off those of others for a short period of time.

Following the death and reported resurrection of Jesus, some of his friends are caught in a maelstrom of confusion, grief and fear. At the end of Luke's gospel, we come across two such friends. This couple are not sitting in an upper room waiting for something to happen; they are walking back from Jerusalem to their home town of Emmaus, seven miles away. While they walk, they talk.

They are telling and re-telling the story, trying to make sense of it, wrestling with how it all came about and where it might lead. There is no internalising of their grief or private reflection on the conundrum of Jesus and his fate. They talk about it while they walk, but find no resolution.

The risen Jesus comes and joins them on their journey. He doesn't tell them to walk a different road or change their direction. He joins them on their journey and accompanies them. He joins them on their territory and engages with them on their terms. As with Peter and Mary Magdalene and others, he starts from where they are and joins them at a place where they are taken with a human and pastoral seriousness and sensitivity. He doesn't confront them or challenge them or make demands of them, testing their commitment and discipleship, but moves himself to the place where they are on safe ground.

It is surely significant of God's priorities that Jesus behaves in this way. Perhaps the question for Jesus is: given who these people are and the experience they have endured recently, how are they going to be enabled to open their minds through the fog of confusion and grief to hear good news and see through a new lens? So he doesn't start with his message of resurrection and beat the friends for their inability to make sense of it. He doesn't demand that they make a leap of faith anyway and sort out the details later. And he doesn't start by talking at them; he joins them, accompanies them, listens to them. In fact, he asks them a question that allows them to express and articulate their own experience and questions without fear of ridicule or correction: 'What are you discussing together as you walk along?' He plays to their strength and sets them

132

free to talk openly. The fact that they don't know who he is only helps them. But it does beg the question that, if they had recognised him, would they have been so free and willing to express their confusion and ignorance? That aside, however, Jesus puts himself in the weaker position (of ignorance) and asks them to tell him what they have been living through and talking about.

The agony of the story makes them stop walking and wonder where this man has been during these last few days and weeks. 'Are you only a visitor to Jerusalem and do not know the things that have happened there in these days?' And instead of removing the embarrassing mask of ignorance and putting himself on firmer ground ('Of course, I know what has been going on – I only asked you to get you talking!'), Jesus asks a further question: 'What things?' They then summarise the story and the problematic nature of it. How, after all, are they supposed to make sense of a man who unites word and action (teaching and healing) in demonstrating the nature of God's kingdom priorities only to find everybody's hopes dashed at the end? What possible connection could there be in someone of messianic pretensions who, instead of liberating the people from their oppression, finds himself nailed to a cross by the emperor's agents? 'We had hoped that he was the one who was going to redeem Israel.' But what a disappointment. And where does this leave us now with our disappointed commitments, shattered and deformed world view, disillusioned hopes for the future, understanding of God and what he is supposed to be doing here? In fact, is God really there at all – and, if he is, is he to be trusted? Or is he just playing games with us? What these friends are saying is that the story doesn't add up; it doesn't make sense. So, how are they to cope with it? Do they have to ditch the whole Jesus thing and regret their gullibility in following him? Or are they missing the point somewhere?

In one sense, Jesus' handling of these people is totally consistent with his handling of most of the people he met in the course of his public ministry. He engages most easily with those who are already questioning. It is those who come to him with a question or a problem who are able to embrace and respond to him. For people whose minds are closed – especially religious conservatives whose minds are rigidly fixed on their single understanding, their 'simple gospel' or 'the plain meaning of scripture' – Jesus was always a bit of a nightmare, and conflict was inevitable as long as he insisted on opening up new questions about their theological assumptions. *Plus ça change*.

Having listened to their account and their bewilderment, Jesus then (and only then) responds. He begins by starkly questioning their reading of the script or, to change the metaphor, by challenging the shape of the lens through which they see the story and make shape out of it. What Jesus doesn't do is to question or refute the events they describe or the predicament in which they find themselves. He suggests, by means of a further question ('Did not the Christ have to suffer these things and then enter his glory?'), that they will now have to listen to a re-telling of the same story that will call for a brave and radical change in language and concept. The story makes perfect sense, but only if the old system is suspended and it is now heard differently.

Cleopas and his friend might well have declined to listen any further at this point. They might have felt that down this road lies heresy and further trouble. They might have held firmly to their original theological framework and only been prepared to hear the story told within it. But, in the event, they didn't. Perhaps Jesus had done to them here what made him both so attractive and infuriating to many of the people he had met during his peripatetic ministry: he had teased their imagination and stimulated their curiosity. Whatever the case, they were now ready to listen and able to hear. Their minds were open to hear the familiar story of God and his people, through the prophets to Jesus, in a new way, a way that made sense of both their theology and their experience. For this is the place where theology and experience can no longer be kept in separate compartments – especially where the motivation might be to keep the theology pure and unharmed, locked and buried where the real world cannot harm it or disappoint its believers. Jesus invites these friends to bring theology and experience together, risking everything, but opening up their minds and lives to new possibilities.

What is clear here is that these friends would have had to re-think and re-imagine what the messianic hope was all about. They would have had to re-read the biblical story through new eyes and decide whether this was so vital that commitment to it, possibly at risk of personal loss, suffering and death, was worth the cost.

It is interesting, however, that words were not enough. There is no indication that before they had reached their destination they had been convinced of the case that Jesus was making. They urged Jesus to stay with them, offering hospitality and care. The text does not allow us to assume that this generosity was a response to the things Jesus had been saying to them. On the contrary, they are simply exercising their conventional cultural obligations in terms of hospitality to the stranger – they are doing nothing more than anyone else in their society would have been expected to do. There is not necessarily anything special here. But Jesus agrees to stay with them and enters their home to share their hospitality.

The sequence of events now is both suggestive and instructive. During their shared meal, Jesus took upon himself the role of host by taking bread, giving thanks and distributing it. And it was only at this point, when action (even ritual) was married to the words they had heard spoken, that 'their eyes were opened and they recognised him'. Words and explanations had not been adequate. A stimulated imagination and satisfied intellect were not enough. But when words and action, word and sacrament, story and event, ideas and matter, experience and symbol are brought together, the picture makes sense both intellectually and emotionally. And so their eyes were opened and they could now glimpse the truth of the story they had heard and the experiences they had shared. And it is only now, at this point, that they realised how their hearts had burned within them while they had walked and talked and listened to Jesus on the road. In other words, it is only later that they could recognise the experience they had had earlier on the journey.

Human behaviour and personality are complex, and people do not respond as quickly or neatly as many of us would like – even to the good news of God's invitation and grace. Fortunately, Jesus starts where we are, on our ground, and allows us the space for the proverbial penny eventually to drop. He doesn't force it or cajole us, but allows us the space to come to terms with what we have heard and seen before deciding what to do with it, how to respond to it, where to go next with it.

So, is it not significant in the telling of these people's story that Jesus disappears as soon as the penny has dropped? He doesn't tell them what to do next or where to go, but leaves them to make their own decisions and take their own responsibility. And here, again, Jesus is totally consistent with his handling of people throughout his public ministry. When the rich young man comes to him with a serious question ('What must I do to inherit eternal life?'), Jesus replies in general terms ('Obey the Commandments ...') and allows the man time to reflect and respond. The young man does so, and Jesus then personalises his response to the man ('Give up your wealth, make yourself vulnerable and interdependent, then you will be able to come and follow me'). When the man declines and goes away sad, Jesus does not run after him or try to compel him in any way. Instead, he lets the man make his own decision and go. Jesus refused to take responsibility for people's discipleship when he was alive and refused to do it after he had been raised from the dead. And there is nothing to suggest that he has changed his behaviour since then – despite the contemporary popular theologies that we can do nothing without his say-so without risking falling into sin. Jesus makes people make their own mind up and take responsibility for the choices they make. And, just in case we try to hang on to him and refer everything to him, he has a habit of disappearing just at the crucial moment when we would want him to hang around. Perhaps it has something to do with God wanting us not just to be 'born again', but also then to grow up.

The interesting thing about Cleopas and his fellow traveller is that they decided to go back to Jerusalem. They could have waited until the safety of the new day and tried to get a good night's sleep. But they did not. Instead, they got up and went back the way they had just come; and, when they got to the place where the closest friends of Jesus were holed up, they told their story and drew their conclusions.

It is a feature of the gospel accounts that Jesus constantly moves people on and refuses to allow himself or their experience of him to be enshrined and venerated. Shepherds descend from the fields around Bethlehem and come to see the newly born baby Jesus, but then are sent back into the fields to continue their work as shepherds. In one sense the world has not changed, but they have changed in the world and return to their familiar lives differently. After his transfiguration on the mountain top, he moves Peter, James and John back down the mountain and on towards Jerusalem. Having disappeared from the home of Cleopas, the friends go back along the same familiar road to a familiar place; but they go back as different people, seeing differently, believing differently, committed to their theological world view differently.

Instead of wanting Jesus to call us out of the familiar and the routine (especially where these are tough or tedious), we often find ourselves sent back into it, but differently. In the same way that prayer is not primarily about changing the world but changing us within the world that already is, so Jesus sends his friends along familiar roads with familiar people, but transformed (or being transformed) by what we have heard, seen and shared with him and his people along the way.

Luke tells us that, while the friends were reporting all this back in Jerusalem, Jesus then appeared in their midst. Again, Jesus acknowledges their fear and suspicion that he is a ghost (so Thomas is not the only 'doubter') before going on to re-tell the story again. He starts at the point at which he finds them, and only then (in fact, having shared food with them – something ghosts don't generally do) does he go on to talk theology. Only when they are at ease and the shock has diminished can he begin to make the connections between their memory of his pre-crucifixion words and actions and their consistency with the Hebrew scriptures. Again he re-tells the story and shines a new light on it, light that might now be able to illuminate what had previously become incomprehensible and might indicate the behind-the-scenes bigger picture of God's activity in and through Jesus. But we should not imagine that this re-telling, consistent though it might be, would have been radically challenging and deeply disturbing to these good Jewish people.

Yet, again, Jesus instructs his friends to stay in the place of threat and fear for a while. They must stay in Jerusalem and not be tempted to run away to a place of greater obscurity or safety. They are not to return to Galilee and the relative security of 'home'. They are not to seek refuge in a place where the memories and associations might be less painful or barbed. They are to stay put and take the time to make sense of all that has happened to them thus far. This they must do here in Jerusalem. They must not try to escape, but do their theology and their praying and thinking and talking in the hard place, the place of fear and threat. Only later, once they have stuck with it and then been able to receive 'power from on high', would they be able to face Jerusalem before going out into the wider world transformed.

These post-resurrection encounters are powerful reminders of what discipleship might mean for us and offer encouragement to those who are open to the risen Christ. Jesus meets us where we are and listens to us – he even asks us questions about ourselves. And this can become the starting point of a conversation in which our questioning and inconsistency are accepted and not ridiculed. He starts from where we are and takes us seriously. He recognises that human beings do not easily change their minds, especially in relation to deeply held assumptions about the way the world is. He meets us at the point when our questioning is acute and our attempts to hold together a credible theology or world view with our experience of the world are most difficult. But, having met us and conversed, offering a new take on the old story, he makes word and action meet – often in symbol and sacrament – before leaving us to make of it what we will. He does not stick around to protect the story and prevent it from being amended, diminished or exaggerated. He lets it go into the hands and minds and souls of fallible human beings and takes the risks that go along with that. Then he lets us take responsibility for what we do with the story, how we live it and with whom we share it. But it is also clear that, having heard, touched and received it, we shall also be judged by it.

If God's activity in creation was to bring order out of chaos, then his activity in Christ is to do the same. These bewildered people have experienced the collapse of a world and the reversal of all that God seems to have promised in creation and the hoped-for redemption of Israel. However, what Jesus does with them in that most gentle and humane way is to bring order out of the chaos of their experience and thinking and believing by re-telling the story differently and re-symbolising God's activity by breaking bread with wounded hands. And so it is that the new order is not really any different from the original order of God's desire, but it has to be heard and seen, symbolised and enacted, offered and received. And, here in the place where chaos and pain have dominated, Jesus takes the chaotic elements and rearranges them to demonstrate how they should be understood and appropriated.

Once again, reflecting on this narrative, we are faced by questions about the church. If the people who bear this Christ's name are to have any credibility, should they not reflect both his nature and priorities? Should the church not be a people marked by grace and humility and the willingness to be thought ignorant or naïve? Should we not meet people where they are and allow them to tell and own their story, however chaotic that story might be? And shouldn't this church be so attentive to the world and its people that it can discern where the chaos and inconsistencies are most painfully experienced and the questioning is most acute in order that this journey can be shared and a story eventually told that will suggest another way of seeing and being? Is this church not called to hold together word and sacrament, proposition and symbol, theology and experience, thus refusing to bow the knee to fantasy theologies or to protect theology from the risks of exposure to the real world? Is this church not invited to accept the hospitality of whoever offers it and on the terms on which it is offered, with gratitude and humility? Are we not called to have the courage to take responsibility for our discipleship in a world from which Jesus has to disappear lest we put him on a static pedestal and worship what has become an idol? And should not the church offer the space and hospitality for people to do their questioning and doubting without fear of rejection or being argued into a corner?

It is evident that many churches do not sing from the same hymn sheet that Jesus sang from. There are churches that build thick walls and have clear boundaries in order to know who is in and who is out. Creeds become base lines of acceptability, and people either have to subscribe to every word or pretend to ... if they are to be allowed to belong. There is a single telling of a single story, and the language and definitions are carefully protected and defended. The call to everybody else to repent (literally, 'change minds') is not reflected in a willingness to continue being converted by hearing a telling of the story that brings a little more order out of the chaos and compels us to live creatively in the light of this story in the world in which God has, presumably, put us. Despite using the language of grace, such a church can be arrogant and exclusive in a way that attracted only harsh condemnation from Jesus.

But there are also churches that are so concerned to be inoffensive that Jesus is turned into a wet liberal westerner who wouldn't dream of upsetting anybody – even the most pharisaical of people. Here there is no cutting edge and little content to the story. Anything goes, and usually nobody comes because it is not clear what one is coming to. There is little point in asking people to do their questioning in the company of a people who then have nothing to say and no coherent story to tell that might bring some order out of the chaos. Such a church might speak of humility and humanity, but, despite its openness and generosity of access, still has no confidence in an articulation and incarnation of the story that is God's.

Thank God there are also churches that reflect the character of God in Christ. Generous and humble, inclusive of whoever encounters them, there is a lack of defensiveness – even about the gospel – and an absence of fear to think and re-think the Christian story. This church demands the space to be creative in the use of word and symbol, insists that its preached theology should be able to stand in the market place, work place or academy. This church creates the space for people to meet the crucified and risen Jesus, starting where they are, not rushing or pushing, but speaking when appropriate (when hearing can actually take place) and telling the story with confidence and grace. Such a church as this refuses to take responsibility for someone else's discipleship or believing, but allows people to grow up and own their own faith and life, continuing their questioning and being free to be honest about their doubts.

This is the sort of church that will be attractive to the sorts of people who found Jesus attractive two millennia ago. It will probably be offensive to the people who found Jesus hard to stomach: the religiously devoted, the theologically rigid and the personally proud.

Chapter 11

SCATTERING

If this was Hollywood, the story would end here. All is well, after all. The horrible people who persecuted Jesus have been embarrassed by his resurrection, and the poor disciples are smiling again after their traumatic experiences. The tears have been wiped away and the future is bright – everyone can live happily ever after.

But this is not Hollywood, and real-life stories never end. They are all always provisional. The resolution of one quandary simply opens the way for confrontation with another. Life is never simple, and endings are never final. So it was for the friends of Jesus, the first Christians.

At the beginning of this book, we noted that God's people are always a journeying people, a pilgrim people. They are constantly on the move, being beckoned by grace to leave and travel and accompany those (not of their choosing) who are also following the call of God. This pilgrim community is shaped not simply by adherence to dogmatic statements about God and the world, but also by their common experience of grace. These are a people who know they have been seen through, are loved and forgiven, called to a new life lived in the company of Jesus and his friends. Having experienced mercy, they cannot be other than merciful to others – whoever they are. These people, in their words, attitudes, values, lifestyle, relationships and behaviour, will look something like the Jesus of the gospels, the one who they claim to be following.

At the heart of their experience will be a God who cannot be pinned down, who will not be tamed or boxed by the manipulations of his people. Remember the Transfiguration and the instinctive desire of Jesus' friends to enshrine their amazing spiritual experience and insight by erecting monuments. Jesus refuses to let them do this and swiftly moves them on down the mountain and towards Jerusalem and all that it will hold for them. They are not to stand and worship; they are to get moving again through the bewildering and challenging world. Even worship is not to be something that distracts them from their journey with Jesus.

The disciples clearly were getting used to the risen Jesus appearing among them, and it is probable that the long period of 'world-view adjustment' was becoming more familiar to some of them. Jesus had told them to stay in Jerusalem for the time being until they had been empowered to move outwards and onwards. Their travels would continue, but only when the *kairos* was upon them and the time was right. So they stayed together and prayed and made sense together of what they had experienced. They were having to make their theology fit their experience and understand their experience theologically.

Jesus had re-told the story of God's activity in the world in a way that re-shaped the world view of the disciples. Now the risen Jesus had committed to them a telling of the story that they in their turn had to own and re-tell in creative ways. Once Jesus had left them and ascended to be with his Father, they were on their own. Yes, they were encouraged and strengthened by the

Spirit who came in wind and fire, but they had to take their responsibility for how they would tell the story and live it out in their world. As they were scattered around the Middle East, Asia and Europe, they encountered new situations that demanded fresh approaches and new questions that had not been considered before. Matters such as circumcision (can you be a Christian without it?) and the consumption of food previously offered to idols (can you be a Christian and eat it?) had to be faced and could not be ducked. But these were new challenges that had not been addressed directly by Jesus and clearly had not formed the subject of a neat paragraph in his theological excursus to Cleopas and his friends on the journey to Emmaus. It is worth slowing down here and looking a little more closely at what happened.

The risen Jesus met a load of his friends on a mountain, spoke with them, then disappeared from their view. With the ascension, the time of direct appearances had come to an end. Once again, just when they were making sense of it all, Jesus left them. Like the friends on the road to Emmaus, just when they are getting it together, he disappears and leaves them to take responsibility for the conclusions which they draw from their own experience of him.

Jesus will not be pinned down. He will not allow himself to be enshrined or enthroned in a place where we can gaze upon him and keep him static. It is regrettable that so much church music attempts to do just that, thus turning worship into an almost intense idol-veneration. It is perhaps ironic that, just when we think we have got him in the right place, he has probably already left and moved on. If the Jesus whom we worship is the Jesus of the gospels, then we might have to take a radical

147

and fresh look at the language which we use and the assumptions that underlie it.

Sometime after the ascension, the friends of Jesus are still together, still trying to make sense of their bizarre experiences. Then Pentecost comes, and with it a remarkable empowerment by God's spirit. This is the point where the penny finally drops in the minds of the disciples and the story finally makes sense. This is, at last, the time when all that they have seen and heard and experienced becomes coherent and consistent, allowing the scales to fall from their eyes and their lens to be re-shaped. Like a blind person removing the bandages and looking for the first time through restored eyes, they are flooded with sense and colour and life. But that isn't the full story.

On the Day of Pentecost, the disciples are together praying when they are disturbed by a sound like a mighty wind and they appear to have tongues of fire upon their heads. Jesus had promised before his death that the Holy Spirit would one day make sense of what they could not comprehend at that point in their story. Jesus had recognised the basic truth that we human beings cannot take on board everything at once, but would have to be allowed to live with contradictions and limited comprehension of truth for as long as it took. He doesn't condemn the disciples for being stupid, heretical or stubborn, but lets them be and simply tells them that one day they will understand. It is the Spirit who would appear once Jesus had finally left them and who would lead them into all truth (that is, the truth about Jesus and what he was about in relation to God and the world). The experience of Pentecost transforms the frightened disciples and empowers them for service. This experience, in making sense of Jesus and his life,

148

compels them to begin to live differently, sharing all that they had by way of food and possessions. Their life together was changed and they formed a new community, a new society. The priorities of Jesus were there to be seen in their care of the poor and the widows. They had finally been shaped by the life and character of Jesus. And isn't that wonderful?

Well, yes it is, but it doesn't quite tell the whole story. The disciples share a new common life, but they are also driven out into the world to tell the story they have experienced and understood. And – God's initiative again – the babble of Babel in Genesis is transformed by the clarity of this good news being understood by all people from all places. The good news of Jesus can no longer be confined by language or culture; the gospel is for all people and may be clearly heard. Of course, the clear hearing is only possible because of the integrity of the people doing the talking and telling the story. The disciples were known and, probably, pitied. Yet here they are, out on the streets, bold as brass, compulsively telling anyone who would listen what they had seen and heard and understood. In other words, in the same way that Jesus had refused to allow his friends to enshrine him and their spiritual experiences and had driven them on into the unknown and uncertain future, so the Spirit does the same. The pilgrim people of God cannot stand still and just bask in the reflected glory of a tamed god.

However, the story doesn't end here either. All the wonderful stuff of the early chapters of the Acts of the Apostles seems to come unstuck in Chapter 5. One couple start to play games with God, and the consequences are not happy. It would be easy to focus on the fate of Ananias and Sapphira and the cause of their demise while missing the bigger point: that already, immediately after Pentecost, despite all the glorious things that have happened, the church – this new community of the redeemed and graced – is still human and flawed and problematic. The Christian community always includes human beings who make wrong decisions, play games, confuse the issues and create a mess. Despite all the good things going on around them, there will always be a certain amount of chaos. That is reality, and that is the church. Thus it always has been and thus it probably always will be … as long as human beings are involved.

This reality is further borne out in the rest of the New Testament accounts. Peter and Paul cannot agree over crucial issues; Paul falls out with his closest friend and associate in mission over a matter of principle; councils are convened to try to resolve matters in a godly way; Christian communities lend their allegiance to competing preachers and evangelists who then try to outdo one another. None of this is commendable, but it is very real. So contemporary Christians need to be a little more humble when using scripture as a tool with which to beat the 'enemy' and a little more honest when telling the story of the early Church. It should always be remembered that some of the most hard-hitting letters in the New Testament were written to address conflict, bad behaviour, un-Christian values and dodgy practices.

This all points us back to the central point here that the early Christian community was quickly sent out into the world to tell the story of Jesus and encourage people to become members of the new fellowship of the graced. They did some remarkable things and made a terrible mess of others. Their story is hopeful and glorious, however, because it is real and honest, eschewing fantasy and propaganda, not having to pretend it was more 'successful' or tidy than it actually was. In its messiness lies its promise of hope.

Writing the fifth act

So, where does this leave us, the church of the twenty-first century in the west? Bishop Tom Wright has conceived of the story of God's people in terms of a five-act play (à la Shakespeare). He helpfully concludes that the fifth act is still being written. The first four acts set out what has been termed 'salvation history' and leave us with the first Christians empowered by the Spirit to continue Jesus' ministry in the world. But the lessons are not over and the challenges not yet fully faced: questions of who the gospel is for (just Jews, or Gentiles too?) have to be faced, and the Christians are split. They have to take the story so far and then make their unprecedented decisions about unprecedented questions in the new world in a way that is consistent with the story so far (as told in the first four acts). Of course, opinion is divided on issues such as whether Gentile converts should have to be circumcised as well as baptised and whether food offered to idols should be eaten for the sake of evangelism. But the challenges cannot be ducked, and the old world cannot be revisited. The temptation to romanticise the old must have been powerful (life seemed simpler then and the dilemmas less difficult – also, other people took responsibility for telling us what to think and how to live).

The church of today faces a similar task: how to continue writing the fifth and final act of God's play in a way that is consistent with the first four acts, but also that grasps the nettles of contemporary and unprecedented questions and dilemmas. This makes the task of theology and ethics difficult, but unavoidable. We are called to be the church now, not to try to recreate the church of 1,000 or 2,000 years ago. We noted earlier that Jesus made people take responsibility for their faith and life, refusing to collude in their desire to take an easier road. Nothing has changed. Christian discipleship, both personal and corporate, forces us into taking responsibility with humility (despite my best theology and intentions, I might have got it wrong) and doing our best with writing the fifth act. We cannot leave it to someone else, and we cannot leave it to God; for God only passes it back to us and tells us not to stay in the comfortable place of spiritual refuge, but to go out into the hard world where the questions are tough and the answers not always clear. The sin is not to have got the answer wrong or the theology out of kilter; rather, it is to refuse to face the questions because they are too hard (or, to borrow the parable referred to in an earlier chapter, to bury the gospel where it can be protected and remain unchallenged).

The first Christians were inescapably innovators. The church of today has no alternative but to be faithful to their tradition in facing with courage questions and dilemmas that have not had to be faced before (including genetics, ecological concerns, technology, human sexuality and identity, even some elements of church shape and order).

The challenge to the first Christians is the same as the challenge faced by Christians of the twenty-first century: how do we hear, understand and own the Christian story in such a way that we can then address confidently and creatively the new (and sometimes unique) challenges and questions of a new world in a way that is consistent with the character and activity of God as seen through history and in the scriptures, experience and life of his people? Furthermore, how can this be done in ways that reflect the generous grace of a God who has a tendency to disappear at the crucial moments in the life and thinking of his people – especially in a world where the experiences and cultural contexts of discipleship for different Christian communities are so diverse? One only has to mention sexuality (especially, but not solely, homosexuality), money and power, and different Christian communities will immediately draw their lines in the sand and build their defences. These are not communities who are especially good at living with provisionality, listening to the genuine questions and experiences of others, or even daring to subject their assumed theologies to any outside scrutiny that might make them have to re-think (or 'repent').

The first Christians were scattered by persecution and their compulsion to tell their story. They quickly founded Christian communities around the then known world. Some of them suffered enormously, and some probably didn't. The Book of Revelation, for example, was written as a visual coded narrative to encourage those facing dreadful persecution, torture and death to stand firm and see their fate in the context of God's story. Christians quickly found that they would always be a pilgrim people, constantly being driven out to unknown and uncertain places and people. Always on the move, unable to pin God down to a place or time or way of being, they went where the Spirit blew them and faced whatever was to come at them when they got there.

Go back to the calling of the first disciples of Jesus. They had no idea where their journey would take them, who was to go with them, how long it would take them to get there or what would happen along the way. And

Jesus didn't tell them either. He consciously dissuaded from following him those who were unlikely to stay the course or were too wedded to their securities to make the journey viable. Nothing has changed. To follow Jesus and to journey with his friends promises the same uncertainty today that it did then. Christian discipleship is not for the 'safe' or the faint-hearted; it is for those who really want to live and experience life in all its edgy fullness. It will require an openness to the world and its hard questions and will demand the sort of humility that costs everything. It is not cheap, but comes at a price. It is also born of grace and sustained by grace, and demands to be exercised with grace.

This is probably the whole point of this book. The Christian Church is founded on grace. Its story, still being written, is about God's gracious love for ordinary and wayward people. It is grace that brings God among us in the flesh and blood of Jesus, and grace that calls people like Mary Magdalene to be a friend of Jesus. It is grace that leads Jesus to a cross and Peter to a hiding place of shame. It is grace that draws the bewildered friends of Jesus to hear the words, 'Don't be afraid'. And it is grace that throws them out into a harsh world, empowered by the Spirit of God, to be responsible for making Jesus touchable in the world. Therefore, it is grace that should characterise the words, behaviour and reputation of Christ's people. The church is called and commanded ('Love one another as I have loved you', says Jesus) to be a proclaimer and embodiment of the good news of God's grace, not a reminder of the bad news of the world's ways.

It will be clear, then, that there is some way to go for the church in the world to become what she is called to be. The language and behaviour of many Christians who disagree with each other demonstrates that grace has not been understood even if it has been experienced. That is the tragedy – tragedy not primarily for the church, but for the world that the church is called to serve.

Telling the story

Even Jesus proclaimed that God's story cannot be suppressed: if people shut up, even the stones will cry out. God will not be silenced and grace will not be extinguished – even by the church. Christian people cannot help but tell the story of God's dealings with them as seen in the light of God's dealings with all people. The Bible bursts with these accounts of people's encounters with this God whose love is eternal and whose desire is to save. As we have noted, the people of God throughout the biblical narrative constantly journey with surprising companions and go to and through places they would rather have avoided. As they journey, they talk and think and reflect. They do their theology as they go, not simply by sitting on it and hoping it can be protected in some arbitrary or convenient pristine condition. They share their experiences with honesty and humility, allowing the light of God and his people to shine on them and illuminate their significance. But, in the end, it all keeps coming back to God and his grace, evidenced particularly in Jesus and now to be incarnated in the church, his called and sent people. And each pilgrim member of this community finds himself or herself compelled to tell their story in the light of God's story to anyone who will listen. It is not a story of achievement and success, and it is not a story designed to boost either the ego or the reputation of the teller. It is a story about how the grace and mercy and love of God, told in so many ways throughout the long history of God's people (as recounted in the Bible), are still experienced now in all their transforming power.

To receive God's grace is to be compelled to live graciously in God's world (and that includes his church). To live graciously is to reflect the character and passion of God himself as seen in Jesus Christ. To do this is to be compelled to articulate in life and word the experience of God in all its bewildering colour. This is both a privilege and a responsibility. For the church of today has to convince a cynical world that it is interested in more than just its own rightness or power. It has to persuade a sceptical world that grace is a reality and that God can be seen among us. It has to demonstrate the self-sacrificial humility that is the only response to God's grace received and comprehended. It must live a common life that does not minimise difference, but holds together those who differ. It must be a community that is called to have its feet washed by its master and its bread and wine blessed by the one who will be betrayed and denied.

It is an enduring mystery how some Christians can arrogantly refuse to share bread and wine with their brothers and sisters in Christ. It is as if we have made the sacraments our own, wresting them from this God of grace who alone can choose with whom he shares his meal. Unfortunately for the arrogant and the self-righteous, Jesus always seemed to eat with those most unlikely to be welcomed at a religious feast and finally re-signified the Passover with friends of dubious character and fickle theological apprehension. If Jesus saw fit to do this with people like Peter and Judas and Thomas, how dare we refuse to commune with those whom Jesus – the Lord of the Supper – has also called? Perhaps the scandal of grace is that grace is scandalously denied to those whom Jesus calls his friends by those who wish to turn grace into a commodity or a badge of acceptability. Pharisees and elder brothers come immediately and unbidden to mind.

The journey continues

Like the disciples of Jesus, our journey does not end. God calls us to move into virgin territory where grace is sometimes rare or absent. Moved by experience and understanding, we are bidden to live and speak God's story and our story wherever we find ourselves and with whomsoever we meet. We do not choose our company, but are compelled to live graciously with those whom Jesus calls to go with him. We are a people who will put up with the provisional behaviours and limited understandings of all sorts of people, exercising the sort of grace Jesus himself showed to unlikely people. The religiously self-righteous will hate it and will find all sorts of ways to put down markers of belonging and conformity. Language will be bent to accommodate their (sometimes unconscious) desire to pin God down and control his friends. But grace will not be beaten.

Indeed, they might succeed in pinning him down on a cross made of their own gracelessness; but God has a tendency to leave crosses and empty tombs behind him, setting people free not to be tied to the decaying and destructive theologies that only imprison and crucify – despite free and confident use of the language of liberation and grace. The Spirit came at Pentecost in forms that cannot be contained or preserved. Wind can be a gentle refreshing breeze on a hot day or a hurricane causing mayhem. Fire can warm up cold bodies and cook good food, but it can also burn down houses and is to be respected. This Spirit cannot be tamed and will blow in the form God chooses and at the time God decides (the *kairos*). It is for God's waiting people to see clearly and discern where the Spirit is at work in the world and to shape the community that bears his name to meet the need appropriately.

Much of this is imprecise and messy. The Spirit cannot be programmed or systematised any more than Jesus could be contained or constrained. The community of God's people will always be a mess as they cast around, marked by their conflicting and partial perceptions of God's call, to live in their world consistently with the story Jesus told. But it will also be messy because the world has not been before where it is today. Jesus expected his surprised friends to let him go, think it all through, then live creatively in their world in a way that was consistent with the story that was now theirs. The call is still ours today. We will be judged on our faithfulness, not to a particular text or image of God, but to the consistency of our character and conduct as a reflection and incarnation of the God who, in Jesus Christ, incarnate, crucified and raised from the dead, upset the arrogant and embraced the humble. We will be judged not by whether we have protected the inheritance by burying it in the garden (away from threat or sight), but by whether we have trusted God enough to risk everything for him, even the loss or re-shaping of the story he has given us.

As Jonah saw, but failed to embrace; as Hosea felt compelled to live out, and bore the cost; as Peter discovered on a walk up the beach: God's grace will not be squashed by the small-minded insecurities and failures of his people. Grace will lead us home because that is who God is and how God is, and God will not be tamed or boxed in a place of our convenience. His Spirit is out and about, blowing where he chooses and inspiring surprising people. If a cross and a tomb could not contain him, his broken church certainly cannot and will not. Grace is abroad in the hearts and minds and experience of those who know themselves to be God's – and that can never be denied or extinguished. It will always be scandalous and surprising, but it will never be contained.

Jesus doesn't call plastic people to be his friends; he calls real people like me. This means living in the world in which he has put me and for which he has called me in such a way that the world might see and believe that what we say about him might just be true. Jesus chose no other way but to use flawed and floundering people like us. He has no illusions about his church and its limited vision, no fantasies about how perfect we might become if only we could ... (please fill in the latest panacea). Jesus was and is a realist. And despite all our inhibitions and pretensions, our shock and incomprehension, he gave himself for us, poured out grace upon us and loves us as a people being open to redemption.

So, there is hope. God is as he is in Jesus Christ. And his pilgrim people, shocked by the scandal of grace, find themselves called to join his party and journey together through the world, both attracting and antagonising by their exercise of generosity and grace, of mercy and acceptance. It has never been any different in the story of God's people. Thank God.

Hungry for Hope

Nick Baines

978-0-7152-0844-1 · £7.99 · Paperback

'If you are anything like me, the following pages will challenge you, stimulate you, and bring you hope.'

Steve Chalke MBE

As a pastor, Nick Baines had to learn the limits of words when accompanying people through their suffering: sometimes silence was the only response. But Nick's understanding of God's engagement with the real world offers genuine hope to suffering people.

SAINT ANDREW PRESS

Speedbumps & Potholes

Nick Baines

Introduction by Sarah Kennedy

978-0-7152-0806-9   •   £8.99   •   Paperback

'Thought-provoking with zest, careful reflection and great fun.'
Rev. Dr Richard A. Burridge, Dean of King's College, London

42 short and entertaining reflections come from observation and the ordinary, everyday experience and offer the reader glimpses of a new perspective on daily life.

'On a blustery cold day, as I write this, Nick Baines has worked his ecclesiastical magic and made me feel much sunnier. And that's a God-given gift'.

Sarah Kennedy, BBC Radio 2

SAINT ANDREW PRESS

Finding Faith

Getting in Tune with God

Nick Baines

978-0-7152-0868-7 · £11.99 · Paperback

We live in a fast-paced, noisy world that seems to get more and more complex and uncertain with every passing year. It's hard to hear your inner voice and to stop and reflect on what life is all about. Where do we find our anchor?

Nick Baines has always found that popular music has offered a rare haven in which it is possible to step back and look at what life is. Throughout his own long journey into faith, there has always been a great song that has helped, encouraged or provided space for reflection at the key moments. In this book, Nick draws on these songs and explores what being a Christian really means. How does it fit with the world in which we live?

SAINT ANDREW PRESS